REVIVAL

PASTOR GREG LOCKE

Global Vision Press™
Mount Juliet, Tennessee

ISBN: 978-1-7358462-7-9

All Scripture taken from the King James Version
of the Holy Bible

Publishing, editing, and cover design by
Global Vision Press and Locke Media

contact@LockeMedia

DEDICATION

I dedicate this book to my 6 beautiful children. My wife Taisha and I have always said that we don't merely want our kids to hear about revival, but actually see it occurring around them. Our church is currently in the midst of an unbelievable move of God, and our children are watching it happen in real time. This alone is one of my greatest joys. Each of my children have come under attack and persecution for simply having me as their father. They each display a remarkable spirit of generosity, and I honor each of them for their courage and loyalty. ***Kiki****, you have an anointing from God that cannot be denied and a fire in your soul that cannot be quenched. Nations will be blessed by your obedience to God's voice.* ***Hudson-Taylor****, the favor of the Lord is upon you, and your ability to articulate the Word of God is astounding. Walk in your God-given authority, and you will change the world.* ***Evan****, the glory of the Lord is rising upon you. You are a warrior who sees into the spiritual realm like few others. Stand and walk in the calling He has placed within you.* ***Malachi****, you are named after a Prophet, and you will walk in a prophetic anointing that will deliver those in the captivity of religious bondage. You have a hidden boldness that will begin to reveal itself and manifest life change in others.* ***Caden****, the Spirit of the Lord is resting upon you in ways that others will not comprehend. You have a wise and discerning heart that will turn multitudes to the truth of Jesus. You are unique and filled with a holy curiosity that will bless each of those around you.* ***Destiny****, you, my little Princess, will be mightily used of the Lord to tear down strongholds and open doors to the supernatural works of God. The enemy seeks to discourage you, but you have the beauty of grace upon you, and you will be used in magnificent worship of the Lord.*

CONTENTS

PREFACE

Years ago, I set out on a journey to understand and explain in simple terms the phenomenon that we call "*revival*". I personally read over 1,000 books on the subject, and I immersed myself in the world of historic awakenings. This book is a small attempt to stir the hearts of everyone seeking a true move of the Spirit of God.

This work is far from exhaustive. Much more can be written, and so much more must be understood. My hope is to reveal what truly "could be" if we earnestly seek a time of refreshing from the Lord. Then it is my prayer that this historical review will ignite an unstoppable movement within the Body of Christ.

~ Pastor Greg Locke

INTRODUCTION

Revival! The very word itself sparks numerous opinions, definitions, and ideas. Questions arise whenever the subject is mentioned. What is revival? How long do revivals last? Can God really send His people revival in these *last of the last days*? Over and over again the questions are asked, but the answers given are seldom Biblical. Please understand that I do not proclaim to be a revival *expert.* Revival cannot be mastered, nor can it be manufactured or manipulated.

No writer, preacher, or historical professor could ever dive the full depth of God's supernatural workings, and this is certainly true when it comes to the sacred subject of revival. The purpose of this small book is not to answer every question about revival, but to expose what begins to take place in the hearts and lives of God's people when it comes—a *time of refreshing from the presence of the Lord.* (Acts 3:19)

In 1774, a young Presbyterian preacher named Samuel Finley preached his most famous sermon in reference to the awakening that was rapidly sweeping the land in his day. His words serve as a powerful introduction to true revival:

> *When he that was formerly a drunkard, lives a sober life: when a vain, light and wanton person becomes grave and sedate: when the blasphemer becomes a praiser of God. When laughter is turned into mourning; and carnal joy into heaviness. When the ignorant are filled with knowledge in divine things, and the tongue that was dumb in the things of God, speaks the language of Canaan: when such*

> *the erroneous are become Orthodox in fundamental points: when such as never minded any religion, do make religion their only business. When busy Martha's and covetous worldlings do neglect their worldly concerns to seek after God's ordinances. Now, these things, and the such like, are discernible to those who are graceless, and according to their own rules they ought to judge that the Devil is cast out, and God has come to His people.*

AMEN! May this short book prepare your heart for all that is to come!

1

A Biblical Example

2 Chronicles 29-31 records the greatest revival that has ever been witnessed. The people of God were living in gross sin, they had forsaken the commandments of the LORD, and had begun to follow many other gods. The state of the people can be clearly seen in the following verses:

> [6]*For our fathers have trespassed and done that which was evil in the eyes of the Lord our God, and have forsaken him, and have turned away their faces from the habitation of the Lord and turned their backs.* [7]*Also they have shut up the doors of the porch, and put out the lamps, and have not burned incense nor offered burnt offerings in the holy place unto the God of Israel.* [8]*Wherefore the wrath of the Lord was upon Judah and Jerusalem, and he hath delivered them to trouble, to astonishment, and to hissing, as ye see with your eyes.*
>
> ~ 2 Chronicles 29:6-8

This historical backdrop sets the stage for the showers of God to fall fresh and anew upon His people. All revivals have been preceded by spiritual degradation and rampant sinfulness. This is a basic fact that both the Bible and world history have proven many times over, and—as we can see in the now famous verse from the same book of the Bible—God is very clear and direct about all He requires before He will let His fire fall on the masses:

> *If my people, which are called by my name, shall humble themselves, and pray, and seek my face, and turn from their wicked ways; then will I hear from heaven, and will forgive their sin, and will heal their land.*
>
> ~ 2 Chronicles 7:14

It's obvious that before God was going to send revival, the people had to start doing that which they had stopped doing. They were not living in a state of humility, but had become proud and arrogant, causing them not to pray to the God of Heaven for their daily needs. They were so busy with their own schedules that they had forgotten to seek the Lord. They were consumed by worldliness and carnality, and God told them that they must repent of their continual wickedness. The simple point is, all spiritual awakenings come after a period—whether short or long in duration—of complete and utter spiritual apathy. This reality should motivate God's people to pray for the God of Heaven to pour out His blessings on this spiritually apathetic and pathetic culture in which we live.

Hezekiah's Revival

The eighteenth chapter of *2 Kings* begins with 25-year-old Hezekiah taking the leadership position as the king of Judah. Immediately we see that he did what was right in the sight of the LORD. With the great burden and responsibility that God had now placed upon him, he knew he must get serious in the service of Jehovah.

> [4]*He removed the high places, and brake the images, and cut down the groves, and brake in pieces the brasen serpent that Moses had made: for unto those days the children of Israel did burn incense to it: and he called it Nehushtan.* [5]*He trusted in the Lord God of Israel; so that after him was none like him among all the kings of Judah, nor any that were before him.*[6]*For he clave to the Lord, and departed not from following him, but kept his commandments, which the Lord commanded Moses.* [7]*And the Lord was with him; and he prospered whithersoever he went forth: and he rebelled against the king of Assyria, and served him not.*
>
> ~ 2 Kings 18:4-7

This is quite a stirring testimony about this great king. God had big things in store for His people, and He was going to use this unusual king to perform the greatest historical awakening that mankind has ever known. There are always undeniable results that join hand in hand with true revival. Every major aspect of genuine revival is mentioned in detail in the account that we will refer to as *Hezekiah's revival*. Although we only have a few brief chapters to draw from concerning this magnificent event, we can clearly see the dynamic impact this movement made upon the people of God. Let's take a look at this divine visitation through eight beautiful perspectives as they played out in the Bible.

A Revival of Sanctification

Any so-called *revival* that does not produce holiness, righteousness, or purity in the participants should be labeled as a *false* or *man-made* revival. Any movement that does not center on a sanctified and separated life is not a movement from Almighty God. This can very easily be seen by reading the account of Hezekiah's revival.

> [4]*And he brought in the priests and the Levites, and gathered them together into the east street,* [5]*And said unto them, Hear me, ye Levites, sanctify now yourselves, and sanctify the house of the Lord God of your fathers, and carry forth the filthiness out of the holy place.*
>
> ~ 2 Chronicles 29:4-5

> [15]*And they gathered their brethren, and sanctified themselves, and came, according to the commandment of the king, by the words of the Lord, to cleanse the house of the Lord.* [16]*And the priests went into the inner part of the house of the Lord, to cleanse it, and brought out all the uncleanness that they found in the temple of the Lord into the court of the house of the Lord. And the Levites took it, to carry it out abroad into the brook Kidron.* [17]*Now they began on the first day of the first month to sanctify, and on the eighth day of the month came they to the porch of the Lord: so they sanctified the house of the Lord in eight days; and in the sixteenth day of the first month they made an end.*
>
> ~ 2 Chronicles 29:15-17

Then they brought twenty-eight animals for sacrifice and reconciliation. The king and the people of the land were indeed interested in cleansing themselves from the wickedness of the world. They realized that God expects holiness from His people. This divine visitation made these people want to live right. They quit their mean and harsh ways and became honest in their business dealings, taking an interest in the house of God. More than anything else, these people wanted to live sanctified lives. They knew that if God was going to continue blessing them, they were going to have to remain set apart from the world. What a blessing to see the people of God desire to live godly lives. When revival comes, holiness and progressive sanctification will always increase among the children of God.

A Revival of Suddenness

In *2 Chronicles 29:36* the Bible gives us one of the clearest definitions of genuine revival. As things were happening in the land and as God was greatly moving upon many hearts, the Lord reveals that, "*Hezekiah rejoiced, and all the people, that God had prepared the people:* ***for the thing was done suddenly.***"

What a beautiful description of a true work of God. Suddenly, out of nowhere, the sovereign, supernatural works of the Lord were being displayed. This was a most unexpected event. There had been no preparation on the part of the people. Hezekiah had not put one article in the local newspaper about a great coming revival. The people did not distribute *revival* flyers that invited people to the house of God at seven o'clock every evening. Nor was a single announcement made over the local radio station.

The Bible says that it was God and God alone that prepared the people for this grand outpouring of grace. Revival fires just quickly began burning and spreading, and there was no time for preparation. Just as it was on the day of Pentecost, the rushing, mighty wind of God's divine presence came in and began to permeate the society.

Oh, how we must understand that revival is a work of God! All the planning and promotion in the world does not promise that our *meeting down at the church* is going to turn into a genuine revival. When revival comes, it will come suddenly! It will be unexpected, undeserved and unannounced. Every major awakening of days gone by came exactly in this fashion—completely out of the blue, with no showmanship involved.

During the 1800's there was a preacher named Charles Finney. He was a remarkable revivalist, yet he saw very little genuine revival. Yes, crowds came, and people were converted, and there was great conviction present in his meetings, but that does not necessarily qualify as being revival. We must realize that conviction and conversion come simply when the Word of God is preached with power. Was Finney a good man? Without a doubt. Was Finney a man with a heartbeat for souls and a passion for spirituality? I most certainly believe that he was. However, his methods of revival were "Charles Finney" methods and not methods produced by the Holy Spirit of God.

Finney's principles of revival and his famous *Lectures on Revival* are most certainly Scriptural and are still greatly used by thousands to this day. However, to say that the methods that he prescribed from the Bible will *definitely* bring about revival is a contradiction to the very essence of genuine revival. God will not—and cannot—be placed in a theological box.

When Hezekiah and the people of God experienced this amazing move of God, the Lord had already prepared them for it, yet they had no idea that it was coming. Should we prepare for revival? Yes! Should we pray for revival? Absolutely! I believe this statement by a preacher of yesteryear puts it plainly: *"Prepare for revival as if it all depended on You. Pray for revival as if it all depended on God. For certainly the latter of the two is the one that is true."*

A Revival of Soul-winning

People coming to know the Lord in salvation is not necessarily evidence of revival. That is the product of evangelism. However, when genuine revival takes place, God's people will be busy about the work of evangelism. Evangelism is always a major outflow of revival. Notice what happened during Hezekiah's revival:

> [1]*And Hezekiah sent to all Israel and Judah, and wrote letters also to Ephraim and Manasseh, that they should come to the house of the Lord at Jerusalem, to keep the passover unto the Lord God of Israel.* [2]*For the king had taken counsel, and his princes, and all the congregation in Jerusalem, to keep the passover in the second month.* [3]*For they could not keep it at that time, because the priests had not sanctified themselves sufficiently, neither had the people gathered themselves together to Jerusalem.* [4]*And the thing pleased the king and all the congregation.* [5]*So they established a decree to make proclamation throughout all Israel, from Beersheba even to Dan, that they should come to keep the passover unto the Lord God of Israel at Jerusalem: for they had not done it of a long time in such sort as it was written.* [6]*So the posts went with the letters from the king and his princes throughout all Israel and Judah, and according to the commandment of the king, saying, Ye children of Israel, turn again unto the Lord God of Abraham, Isaac, and Israel, and he will return to the remnant of you, that are escaped out of the hand of the kings of Assyria.* [7]*And be not ye like your fathers, and like your brethren, which trespassed against the Lord God of their fathers, who therefore gave them up to desolation, as ye see.* [8]*Now be ye not stiffnecked, as your fathers were, but yield yourselves unto the Lord, and enter into his sanctuary, which he hath sanctified for ever: and serve the Lord your God, that the fierceness of his wrath may turn away from*

you. [9]For if ye turn again unto the Lord, your brethren and your children shall find compassion before them that lead them captive, so that they shall come again into this land: for the Lord your God is gracious and merciful, and will not turn away his face from you, if ye return unto him. [10]So the posts passed from city to city through the country of Ephraim and Manasseh even unto Zebulun: ***but they laughed them to scorn, and mocked them. [11]Nevertheless divers of Asher and Manasseh and of Zebulun humbled themselves, and came to Jerusalem.***

~ 2 Chronicles 30:1-11

Here we have a rather lengthy explanation of what took place when the fires of God began to fall. They didn't want to keep these great blessings to themselves—nor were they able to. They just had to go out and let other people know about the merciful God of Heaven. The king sent out all of his postmen to deliver messages to all of their neighbors round about. They were emphatically inviting them to come to Jerusalem to see the mighty works of God. As God began working in their hearts as a nation, they became greatly concerned and burdened for those who did not know Jehovah God, and for those that had forsaken Him—the God of their fathers. The Bible tells us that many of them were mocked for the sharing of the message.

However, in the midst of this mockery, many of these dear people humbled themselves and came to Jerusalem for repentance and worship. Genuine revival has a way of making God's people see their huge responsibility of sharing the message of the grace of God with a lost and dying world. "*Let the redeemed of the LORD say so*" (Psalm 107:2).

In times of revival, our eyes are taken off of our selfish plans and placed upon those who are outside the fold of Heaven. True conversion will be greatly apparent during times of real refreshing. *The Great Commission* will be enthusiastically obeyed by the saints of God, as we will be overwhelmed with the *lostness* of man's condition without Jesus Christ.

People who have not spoken about their faith in years will suddenly sense the overwhelming burden to be faithful witnesses to those whom they come in contact with on a daily basis. We too will suffer mockery and ridicule, but those who truly r*epent and believe the Gospel* will make all the scorning very much worthwhile. How we should endeavor to go great lengths for the never-dying souls of humanity. When real revival comes, then real evangelism will follow.

A Revival of Sensitivity

As the context of the chapter continues, Hezekiah realizes that the people have transgressed the law of God, and his heart is overwhelmed with the fact that God would judge the people.

> [18]*For a multitude of the people, even many of Ephraim, and Manasseh, Issachar, and Zebulun, had not cleansed themselves, yet did they eat the passover otherwise than it was written. But Hezekiah prayed for them, saying, The good Lord pardon every one* [19]*That prepareth his heart to seek God, the Lord God of his fathers, though he be not cleansed according to the purification of the sanctuary.* [20]*And the Lord hearkened to Hezekiah, and healed the people.*
>
> ~ 2 Chronicles 30:18-20

Revival brought about a sensitive spirit in the leadership. However, it also brought a great deal of sensitivity to God's people as a whole.

> [22]*And Hezekiah spake comfortably unto all the Levites that taught the good knowledge of the LORD: and they did eat throughout the feast seven days, offering peace offerings and* ***making confession to the LORD God of their fathers.*** [23]*And the whole assembly took counsel to keep other seven days:* ***and they kept other seven days with gladness.***

~ 2 Chronicles 30:22-23

What was it that was happening? God Himself had come down, and the people did not want their wicked sin anymore. They began to confess openly their sins against God, *and sin wasn't welcome any longer.* It grieved them that they had grieved God.

This is always a true mark of revival. The tides of iniquity will be squelched during seasons of refreshing. Confession will be made. Forgiveness will be received. The people will be disturbed over their sin. A sensitive spirit will become evident throughout the entire land.

Without a doubt, America is one of the most insensitive places on the face of God's earth. Everywhere we look we see the uncaring, un-compassionate lifestyles among the saved and unsaved alike, but revival will bring about a unique sensitivity to the things of God to ensure we're ready for all that is to come.

The people of Hezekiah's day were so overwhelmed with their sin, that not only did they confess their sins, but they actually wanted this manifestation from the LORD to continue in their hearts. When it comes, the cry of revival will be, *bend me, break me, mold me and make me.*

Sensitivity will always hold hands with true God-sent revival.

A Revival of Singing

During the midst of this divine visitation, a most remarkable thing began to happen. As Heaven came down, the Bible tells us that the people of God started to sing the mighty praises of God.

> [27]*And Hezekiah commanded to offer the burnt offering upon the altar.* ***And when the burnt offering began, the song of the LORD began also*** *with the trumpets, and with the instruments ordained by David king of Israel.* [28]*And all the congregation worshipped,* ***and the singers sang****, and the trumpeters sounded: and all this continued until the burnt offering was finished.* [29]*And when they had made an end of offering, the king and all that were present with him bowed themselves, and worshipped.* [30]*Moreover Hezekiah the king and the princes commanded the Levites* ***to sing praises unto the LORD*** *with the words of David, and of Asaph the seer.* ***And they sang praises with gladness, and they bowed their heads and worshiped.***
>
> ~ 2 Chronicles 29:27-30

Then in *2 Chronicles 30:21*, we read, "*…and the Levites and the priests praised the LORD day by day, singing with loud instruments unto the LORD.*" This was the same phenomena that characterized the great Welsh Revival of 1904-1906. At that time, singing became the norm of the day. Praise to God was freely offered by the hearts of those that had experienced these marvelous blessings of revival. No song leader was needed, and in most cases, a hymnal was nowhere to be found—just the simple adoration of praise and humility.

In contrast, it's evident that *American Christianity* has a BIG problem. It is far too *American* and not enough *Christian.* It would be more fitting to call it *American Churchianity.*

We simply *play* too much church. Our buildings are full of blatant hypocrisy. Most of our song services are a waste of time and a complete disgrace to Almighty God. Our hearts are so full of the world's debauchery that we can't enjoy the *songs of Zion.* Let it be dogmatically announced, that when the Heaven-sent living Holy Ghost makes Himself known, heartfelt revival falls from Heaven and *the saints of God WILL sing to the glory of their God* (Psalm 149:5).

According to the Bible, when a person is truly filled with the Spirit of God, they will be singing and making melody in their hearts to the Lord (Ephesians 5:19). Oh, how we desperately need a renewal of old-fashioned singing in the heart, in the home, and in the house of God.

A Revival of Spreading Excitement

The Bible also tells us that—like a well-winded prairie fire—the flames of God's power swept through the land with magnificent force. It swept through every home, every working establishment, and every school. The entire kingdom was in the midst of a sweeping spiritual awakening. Let's look at the continual impact that this r*evival meeting* had upon all who were involved.

> [25]*And all the congregation of Judah, with the priests and the Levites, and all the congregation that came out of Israel, and the strangers that came out of the land of Israel, and that dwelt in Judah,* ***rejoiced.*** [26]***So there was great joy in Jerusalem: for since***

the time of Solomon the son of David king of Israel there was not the like in Jerusalem.

~ 2 Chronicles 30:25-26

There had never before been such a great impact upon these people. The LORD God Almighty came down and no one needed another person to tell them. *It was evident.* Joy was everywhere. The people of God were in a *constant* state of rejoicing. It spread so far and so fast that the people were absolutely amazed at the power of God. It was unexplainable. It was unbelievable. It was uncontrollable. And—more important—it was also *unforgettable* and *undeniable.*

These people knew that they were in the presence of God, and it excited them to no end. They could not control themselves. They could no longer hold it in their hearts. In *Psalm 85:6,* the sons of Korah wrote, "*Wilt thou not revive us again: that thy people may rejoice in thee?*" It was obvious in that day that rejoicing had ceased, and drudgery had set in. They prayed for revival for one simple reason: "*.... That thy people may rejoice in thee.*"

According to God's Holy Word, when there is no joy, there is no real revival. Most of our churches are empty, hollow, shallow, and dry as last year's bird's nest. There is no real substance. As the Apostle Paul wrote, we "*...have a form of godliness but deny the power thereof.*" (2 Timothy 3:5) However, during times of revival, we will experience a new peace and a new joy. Our fellowship with Christ will be greatly strengthened. Our faithfulness to God's Word, God's House, and God's people will be increased. We will have an unceasing desire to "*Grow in grace and in the knowledge of our Lord and Saviour Jesus Christ.*" (2 Peter 3:18)

Every revival that has ever taken place has had the characteristic of spreading out and furthering the message of God's Word. Individuals, communities, churches and nations are changed for the better. That's why it's called revival. It is a return to the great truths of God. It awakens us to our spiritual slumber and causes us to realize the gravity of our responsibilities within the will of God. What a dynamic phrase, "*…there was not the like in Jerusalem.*" (2 Chronicles 30:26)

They had no trouble differentiating between man's work and God's work, as the contrast was incomparable. They knew that this was not how things had been in the past. So they waited with anticipation to see if it would continue into the future.

A Revival of Sacrifice

A careful examination of the text of Scripture will reveal that when the revival came, the people gave up on their stingy, selfish ways. They finally understood that God commands a life of dedication and sacrifice from His children.

> [5]*And as soon as the commandment came abroad, the children of Israel brought in* ***abundance*** *the firstfruits of corn, wine, and oil, and honey, and all the increase of the field;* ***and the tithe of all things brought they in abundantly.*** [6]*And concerning the children of Israel and Judah, that dwelt in the cities of Judah, they also brought in the tithe of oxen and sheep, and the tithe of holy things which were consecrated unto the LORD their God,* ***and laid them by heaps.*** [7]*In the third month began they to lay the foundation of the* ***heaps****, and finished them in the seventh month.* [8]*And when Hezekiah and the princes came and saw the* ***heaps****, they blessed the LORD, and his people Israel.* [9]*Then Hezekiah questioned with the priests and the Levites concerning the* ***heaps****.* [10]*And Azariah the chief priest*

of the house of Zadok answered him, and said, Since the people began to bring the offerings into the house of the LORD, we have had enough to eat, ***and have left plenty****: for the LORD hath blessed his people; and that which is left is this great store.* [11]*Then Hezekiah commanded to prepare chambers in the house of the LORD; and they prepared them,* [12]*And brought in the offerings and the tithes and the dedicated things* ***faithfully****...*

~ 2 Chronicles 31:5-12

The people had been holding out on God for many years. When revival came, they got their hearts right in the sight of God and began to sacrificially give to the work of the Lord. They were well aware of the fact that God had commanded the tithe and the numerous freewill offerings of the heart. However, they had forsaken God's law and had become self-centered and disobedient. I believe the reason most people in our day do not want revival is simply because they're too wicked and stingy with their finances. If God has someone's heart, He will also have no trouble getting to their wallet.

One thing is for sure: *There will be* ***NO*** *God robbers during times of spiritual awakening.* These people got serious about their responsibilities. We must understand that God does not merely own ten percent of our money. According to the inerrant Word of the Living God, He owns all of our money. During times of spiritual renewal, people gain a fresh sense of God's ownership. They will begin tithing. They will begin to help others in their financial battles. Generosity and sacrifice will flood the house of the Lord. The people of God will have no problem understanding and practicing the principle of *Luke 6:38*, "*Give and it shall be given....*" That said, be assured that money is not the only area of sacrifice that true revival brings about, but it is certainly one of the greatest litmus tests to its genuineness.

A Revival of Sound Doctrine

The closing remarks that we have concerning this great visitation from God are recorded in the conclusion of the thirty-first chapter of *2 Chronicles*:

> [20]*And thus did Hezekiah throughout all Judah, and wrought that which was good and right and* ***truth*** *before the LORD his God.* [21]*And in every work that he began in the service of the house of God,* ***and in the law, and in the commandments****, to seek his God, he did it* ***with all his heart*** *and prospered.*
>
> ~ 2 Chronicles 31:20-21

Hezekiah had a heartbeat, and he passed that heartbeat on to the people of God. That passion was to do things in accordance with the Word of God. He desired complete truth, and this mighty wind of revival was enough to remove the breezes of liberalism and modernism in his heart. These people had now experienced firsthand the changing power of God's Word, and they were not about to compromise their stand upon it.

We are living in a day when doctrine is a dirty word, and love is the key to breaking through this aversion and unlocking the mysteries of God's Word. May it go down in history as being simply and straightforwardly said: ***Any movement that forsakes Bible doctrine is most certainly NOT A movement of GOD!*** Doctrine is not a unifier. It is divisive, and it is designed to be so. Be reminded of the Lord's sobering words recorded in the *Gospel of Matthew*, where Jesus said, "*Think not that I am come to send peace on earth: I came not to send peace, but a sword.*" (Matthew 10:34)

If we're going to be truly hungry for Holy Spirit revival, we're going to have to be serious about Bible doctrine. Genuine revival has always brought about reverence and obedience to holy doctrine. As a matter of fact, Hezekiah sought the *truth* with all his heart. May we too see this great need to examine the doctrines of the inspired Bible that we say we so dearly love. True revival will **ALWAYS** exalt right, correct, and sound doctrine.

> *For the word of God is quick, and powerful, and sharper than any two-edged sword, piercing even to the dividing asunder of soul and spirit, and of the joints and marrow, and is a discerner of the thoughts and intents of the heart.*
>
> ~ Hebrews 4:12

2

What The Bible Says...

Having studied what the Bible teaches us about Hezekiah's amazing revival, it's important to realize that one single teaching—whether preached from a pulpit or typed on the written page—can never do justice to the subject of this book. For this, it's essential to understand the fundamental principles of Biblical revival. In hopes that your spirit has been aroused and renewed by this heartwarming story of divine intervention, let's proceed—with prayer and expectation—in hope that God will open our hearts to the desperate need of the hour: *Revival from Heaven.*

We'll start with a brief review of the basic Biblical terminology. The term *revival* has been an often used and much abused term in modern Christianity. The word revival is frequently referred to as an evangelistic crusade or a series of meetings in a local church. While these and many other happenings can align when real revival comes, they're not at all what the word *revival* suggests in regard to Scripture.

The actual word revival is never even mentioned in the Bible. However, the word *revive* is used on various occasions. The Psalmist prayed, "*Wilt thou not revive us again that thy people may rejoice in thee?"* (Psalm 85:6) The wording here would indicate that at one time there was a better condition of living than the present. To revive, then, would simply mean to restore or rekindle.

The actual word revival is of a rather recent origin. Richard Owen Roberts, in his edited work, *Scotland Saw His Glory*, had this to say about the word's meaning:

> *It's earliest appearance in this sense, according to the Oxford English Dictionary, is to be found in the Magnalia Christi Americana of Cotton Mather, published in 1702. It is important to note that although we are not aware of any writers using the word "revival" before Cotton Mather, the blessing itself was much in the minds of American writers prior to him. They were greatly concerned about the condition of the church in their day and frequently used such expressions as the effusions of the Spirit, the necessity of reformation, returning unto God, the wonderful works of God.*

Revival versus Revivalism

One must be careful not to confuse the terms *revival* and *revivalism.* Revival is what God does *for* His people. Revivalism is what God does *through* His people. John H. Armstrong, in his book *When God Moves,* defined it this way:

> *Revivalism....it's people attempting to bring about a work of God. It will produce clouds without rain. It will feed the church with cotton candy, when only real food can bring life and lasting godliness.*

Without a doubt, true revival is both desirable and beneficial, but if we keep associating revival with revivalism, we will end up being content in all the wrong ways. We'll in turn rob God of the glory that we're required to give Him. There are many passages in the Word of God that use *revival terminology*, and most— if not all—are self-explanatory.

> *Oh that thou wouldest rend the heavens, that thou wouldest come down, that the mountains might flow down at thy presence…*
>
> ~ Isaiah 64:1

In this verse in Isaiah, revival is referred to as *rending the heavens*. A careful study of this full passage will reveal that Isaiah did not pray for God to rend the earth or the people. When something begins to happen in the Heavens, it is always manifested upon the earth. When the sun is at its brightest and the wind ceases to give off its unseen breath, the people outside feel complete misery and discomfort as they search for shade. When the Heavens pour forth in unceasing torrents of rain, the ground below becomes flooded, and great disasters can and have occurred. When snowflakes begin to drift from the sky, it isn't long until the land below is blanketed with *white death* which can either be a delight for frolicking children or completely paralyze an entire city.

When God begins to do His rending and tearing of the Heavens, it will not be long until it is greatly felt below the Heavens. Oh, how we need God to rend and tear our hearts! The prophet Isaiah continues in the same passage and pleads for God to *come down* amongst His people. Real revival is nothing more than the LORD God of Heaven, creator of all life, coming down in the midst of His people in great power and glory.

Awakening

Another brief Bible definition of revival would be that of an *awakening*. This term is used in regard to the First Great

Awakening of 1730-1760 and the Second Great Awakening in 1800-1830. The actual word can be found a number of times in Scripture, but the Apostle Paul makes it clear as to the Biblical meaning.

In *1 Corinthians 15:34* Paul wrote, "*Awake to righteousness and sin not...*". If one were to be honest with the text, it's quite evident that an awakening is nothing more than realizing a state of wickedness and waking up to the fact that man has offended Holy God and must repent for the sake of righteousness. God has always put a premium upon personal holiness and righteous living. When true revival comes, it will produce a spirit of *doing right and being right* amongst God's people.

In *Hosea 10:12*, the prophet Hosea is calling a rebellious and backslidden nation back to Jehovah God through the avenue of inspiration when he says: "*Sow to yourselves in righteousness, reap in mercy;* ***break up your fallow ground:*** *for it is time to seek the LORD, till he come and rain righteousness upon you.*" The phrase "*break up your fallow ground*" has the idea of a stony, cold and indifferent heart that is in much need of repentance and rekindling.

Without a doubt, the most fulfilling Bible definition on the subject of revival is found in *Acts 3:19*, where the Apostle Peter, filled with the Holy Spirit, is preaching to the men of Israel and boldly declares, "*Repent ye therefore, and be converted, that your sins may be blotted out, when* ***the times of refreshing*** *shall come from the presence of the Lord*" Our churches today are in desperate need of a supernatural refreshing from the hand of Almighty God.

What Others Have Said
Concerning *revival*, RA. Toney had this to say:

> *A revival is a time when God visits with His people, and by the power of the Holy Spirit imparts new life to them, and through them imparts life to sinners. Revivals are not religious excitements stirred up by the cunning methods and the hypnotic influence of the mere professional evangelist.*

J. Edwin Orr defines it this way:

> *Spiritual awakening is a moment of the Holy Spirit bringing about a revival of New Testament Christianity in the church of Christ and its related community.*

Stephen F. Olford went on to say:

> *Revival is the sovereign act of God in which He restores His own backsliding people to repentance, faith and obedience.*

Charles G. Finney said:

> *Revival presupposes that the church is sunk down in a backslidden state, and revival consists in the return of the church from her backslidings and reaping the harvest of souls.*

Andrew Murray defined it this way:

> *The true meaning of the word (revival) is far deeper. The word means making alive again. Those who have been alive but have fallen into what is called a cold or dead state. They are Christians and*

> *have life, but they need reviving to bring them back to their first love again. The healthy growth of the spiritual life to which conversion was meant to be the entrance.*

Richard Owen Roberts has said:

> *Revival is a time when Heaven comes closer to earth than at any other time in the lives of men and women. It is the extraordinary movement of the Holy Spirit that produces extraordinary results.*

Henry C. Fish gives this definition:

> *Revivals are seasons when Christians are waked to a more spiritual frame, to more fervent prayer, and to more earnest endeavors to promote the cause of Christ and redemption; and consequent upon this, seasons when the impenitent are aroused to the concerns of the soul and the work of personal religion.*

James Alexander Stewart said:

> *Revival means a fresh incoming of the Divine Life into a body that is threatening to become a corpse.*

And finally, DL Moody said, in no uncertain terms:

> *Revival is a return to Bible Truth.*

No matter the description, it is quite evident that a genuine revival is exactly what we need today. Modern society is ever-changing, and that change is not for the better. There seems to be a diabolical stream of corruption flowing from the White House down to the church house.

People, pride, and programs keep *most* Christians from their sacred responsibilities. Sins of the flesh, as well as sins of the spirit, choke the very life from our evangelical churches. If there is anything that is needed in this fast-paced world of madness, mayhem, and materialism, it is unreservedly a "t*ime of refreshing from the presence of the Lord.*"

The great preacher Charles Spurgeon once said, "*What we need is a revival of powerful preaching, old-fashioned doctrine, fervent prayer, personal godliness, domestic devotions and genuine love.*" If one were to study a complete listing of revival related terminology, they would find words and phrases such as: divine visitation, divine manifestation, glory, Pentecost, quickening, revealing, rekindling, fire from Heaven and a host of others.

There are an estimated 10,000 books that have been written on the subject of revival. This great number of books would explain the broad diversity of definitions that have been given to this remarkable word and the phenomenon it represents. Simply stated, *revival is nothing more than the sovereign, supernatural and spontaneous working of God whereby Christians are awakened to the holiness of God, the sinfulness of themselves and the eternal damnation of the lost.*

Conditions That Precede Revival

A thorough study of the history of revivals will conclude that every major revival that has ever taken place, came under conditions that were less than desirable. Spiritual declension and apostasy run rampant before a move of God begins. This decline of morals in individuals and in society is not what necessarily sparks a revival of religion, but it is used to bring people to the understanding of such a need.

The very fact that conditions before revival are not meeting God's standard of holiness, proves that real revival is an awakening in the heart and a renewing of the mind (Psalm 85:6; Romans 12:2). In regard to the times that preceded the First Great Awakening in America, the Rev. Charles L. Thompson of Chicago made the following observation:

> *The difference between the Church and the world was vanishing away. Church discipline was neglected, and a growing laxness of morals was invading the churches. The young were abandoning themselves to frivolity and amusements of dangerous tendency, and a party spirit was producing its natural fruit of evil among the old.*

As we study the historical significance of revivals in the Bible, we'll find—without much searching—that a spirit of declension and looseness characterized God's people before He sent them a revival blessing. Many passages in Scripture record that God referred to His people as spiritual adulterers and stubborn animals. He called them to repentance and then "*poured out the water upon dry ground.*" (Isaiah 44:3)

History reveals that from the New Testament Church age until the early fifteen-hundreds, the Church had lost much, if not most of its influence. The Roman Catholic Church had silenced the mouth of many a preacher and executed anyone who opposed its pagan traditions. This period of time has often been described as the *dark ages of the church.* Then, as a reminder of God being in complete control, He raised up a mouthpiece for the Reformation.

On October 31, 1517, Martin Luther nailed a copy of his Ninety-Five thesis to the door of the Castle Church in Wittenberg, Germany. The Lord used this bold step of faith to spark the revival and return to the doctrines of the Word of God. While revival is an awakening of heart, reformation is a revival of the discovery and return to the truth.

Before the great Laymen's Prayer Revival of 1857-1858, there were twelve consecutive years of moral, social, economic, and spiritual decline. Many years after the revival had subsided, Mr. C.L. Thompson recounted the condition of the land before God, "*...moved upon the face of the waters.*" He said:

> *It was a time of reckless expenditures, of unparalleled fervor for riches without much consideration of how they were obtained, of an apathetic conscience and a wakeful selfishness, of a coldness and deadness in the Church, and an alarming godlessness outside of it. The nation seemed to be drifting in the same direction in which it had gone before the great revivals of 1800. Skepticism pervaded all ranks of society. We were becoming a people without God in the world.*

Revival in the Last Days

Almost every state in America has experienced revival blessings since 1790. America, as a nation, has not seen a major revival in over one hundred years. This, however, does not mean that America can't or won't see a mighty move of God. *Malachi 3:6* states, "*For I am the LORD, I change not....*" *Hebrews 13:8* goes on to say, ... "*Jesus Christ is the same yesterday, today and forever.*" The same God that has sent revivals in the past, is the same God that can send revivals in the present—and in the future.

It is true that America is a sin-sick nation that has fallen farther in debauchery than any preceding nation in the world, but the sovereign God that has all-redeeming grace has all-reviving grace as well. It can't be proven that God will revive America in these last days, but it also can't be proven that He will not. *The issue is not whether He will send revival, but rather that He* ***CAN*** *send revival.* In his book *Revival, The Need And Possibilities,* C.C. B. Bardsley described the early 1900's this way:

> *The authority of the Bible is openly questioned, the Church is worldly and materialistic, the world is self-centered and pleasure mad, the home is rapidly breaking down, society is being imperiled by defiance of moral sanctions, and crime is rampant and flagrant.*

Furthermore, in his book *Give Him No Rest: A Call To Prayer For Revival,* Erroll Hulse said the following:

> *We must not forget the situation that preceded the eighteenth-century awakening. We have liberalism; they had deism. We have the drug menace; they had rum. We have abortion; they had the degradation of the slave trade. We have contempt for the Gospel, especially in places of influence; so did they.*
>
> *We have bishops who tolerate practicing homosexuals in the ministry and the blatant public denial of the deity of Christ by one of their number; eighteenth-century Britain also suffered a supine clergy. Yet in spite of all the obstacles, the Holy Spirit intervened in a marvelous way, using the humble prayers and a handful of godly leaders. The spiritual condition of the Church and the world today should drive believers to their knees to beseech the throne of Heaven, "Do it again Lord, do it again."*

The Objects of Revival

In many instances, revival has been greatly confused with evangelism. If we attend special services or a series of meetings where several professions of faith are made, it is usually stated that revival has occurred. Without a doubt, people will be saved when genuine revival comes. However, people being saved and *born again* is not *in and of itself* revival. Revival is strictly to be experienced by *God's people*—the *objects* of true revival. The evangelization of the lost is a proper outflow of a move of God, but even evangelism will not happen in truth when there is no atmosphere of Holy Spirit power.

Hospitals have a mandatory cleaning routine for all of their nursery facilities. Everything is in its proper place, and all instruments must be kept very clean. This isn't for the physician's benefit, but for a conducive atmosphere to the birthing of babies. The same is true in the Church. The Lord must send us times of conviction and divine manifestation to humble and purify our hearts in order to create an atmosphere for the birthing of spiritual babies into the Kingdom of God. Leonard Ravenhill said, "*Revival is when God comes to the aid of His sick Church.*" Let's be clear that every passage of Scripture that deals with the subject of revival is addressed to believers alone. A preacher of the past made the following statement: "*Christians are more to blame for not being revived than sinners are for not being converted.*"

Lost people aren't in need of a revival or a rekindling of the heart because there is not yet anything in them to revive. In contrast, those who are without Christ need to be raised from their spiritual graves. The Bible declares that the unsaved are *dead in trespasses and sins* (Ephesians 2:1).

Before one can experience an awakening, they must first experience a quickening of their dead spirit by the Holy Spirit of God—they must be *born again*. The Lord designs revival for the specific purpose of bringing His people back into a zealous and loving relationship with

Himself. When this is accomplished, then, and only then, will sinners truly be turned unto the Lord.

> *Jesus answered and said unto him, Verily, verily, I say unto thee, Except a man be born again, he cannot see the kingdom of God.*
>
> ~ John 3:3

3

Major Themes of Revival

There are certain themes and issues that are prevalent in every genuine work of revival. God uses each to bring about and sustain a revival. In the following pages, I'll review each of the six distinct themes.

Holiness vs. Sinfulness

The first of these themes would be the *holiness of God and the sinfulness of man*, which is the hallmark of any outstanding work of God. In the book of Isaiah, we see a prophet that pronounces woeful judgment on an entire nation for three complete chapters of Scripture. Eight times he *woes* them for their wickedness.

There are seven classes of people that Isaiah pronounced judgment upon. In his classes, the drunkards received two woes from this prophet of God.

Then, in chapter six, Isaiah saw a vision of a thrice-holy God upon an exalted throne. He saw God in all of His majesty, glory and splendor. Immediately, the prophet stopped his hard preaching to the nation and proclaimed *himself* to be sinful and vile. What could provoke such a reaction in the heart of Isaiah? It was nothing more than the absolute holiness of God.

In real seasons of revival, man will see himself for whom he really is and will see God in all His holiness. He will realize that God is his only hope of life and breath. The holiness of God *is* the measuring rod of all revivals. Throughout the Bible, we're repeatedly told of the absolute holiness of God. Yes, God is love, but His love is a holy love. We're also told God is wonderfully merciful, but His mercy is a holy mercy.

We sing of God's Amazing Grace, but we must never forget that His grace is a holy grace. We expound upon the great power of God, but this power is without a doubt a *holy* power. If God were not loving, if He had no mercy, if He showed no grace, and if He were completely powerless, *He would still be holy*.

Holiness is *everything* that God is, and He could never be anything less. Each one of the sixty-six books of the Bible proves the holiness of God. The God of Scripture has no desire for anything that is not holy. This is exactly the reason that unholy man must be made holy by the precious blood of Jesus Christ. If the holiness of God is not exalted on the lips and in the life, one can be assured that what is taking place is not a genuine revival of religion.

In recent days, there has been much talk of so-called "*revivals*" across the nation and around the world. These revivals are usually confined to those of the charismatic denomination or persuasion. A proper study of these movements will reveal that all kinds of foolishness and un-Scriptural events are often seen in these movements.

You'll hear of people falling on the ground with unstoppable laughter and in some instances barking like dogs. Maybe this is legitimate, but I tend to believe it often is not. When the nation's leading *healing evangelists* pray for the people in their congregation, the subjects frequently fall backward to the ground simply because the evangelist pushed them or otherwise manipulated them to do so.

In contrast, an in-depth study of God's Word will reveal that those who came into the true presence of God fell on their faces at His very humbling holiness. The only group of people that are recorded in Scripture as having fallen backward, were the soldiers that came to arrest Jesus in the garden. I trust you see the difference. *Foolishness is not acceptable in the presence of holiness.*

For a detailed study on this modern *revival phenomenon,* read Hank Hanagraf's book entitled, *Counterfeit Revival*. When real Heaven-sent, heart-felt, Holy Ghost revival comes, the subjects of this moving will be on their faces before a God who is intrinsically holy. Dr. Rod Bell, long time pastor of the Tabernacle Baptist Church in Virginia Beach, Virginia, had the wonderful privilege of seeing God's hand of mercy graciously visit his church with revival in 1992.

In his *Reflections Of Revival*, he said, "*With my heart as wicked as it is, how could a holy, sovereign God breath upon us? I feel so sinful, I feel so wicked. I feel so unclean. I must express my feeling. I feel so unworthy, I feel as though I am the chief amongst sinners. Knowing what I know about myself and then realizing that God knows so much more about me than I know, I am so unworthy of this divine breath of Heaven. But then, so are we all."*

The men God saw fit to use in all major revivals of the past, were men that fervently preached on the holiness of God. Jonathan Edwards famous sermon, *Sinners In The Hands of An Angry God,* was full of references to God's holiness. God is just in anything that He does. Even in allowing sinners to be condemned to Hell. The simple fact that God is holy proves that He will never tolerate sin. When men understand the true holiness of God, they're made to tremble in deep conviction.

The preaching, singing, fellowship and overall atmosphere during seasons of revival will always be saturated with the *complete* holiness of God and the utter depravity of man.

True Repentance

The second theme that is found woven throughout the history of revival is that of *repentance.* Regardless of denominational preference or theological background, nearly every author that has written on the subject of revival has eventually come to the conclusion that repentance is an essential clement in a divine visitation from God.

Repentance does not cease when a sinner is converted to Christ. True and Biblical repentance is worked out in the life (Philippians 2:12). On several occasions, Jesus told His Church to repent. To the church of the Laodiceans He said, "*As many as I love I rebuke and chasten, be zealous therefore and repent.*" (Revelation 3:19) In *2 Chronicles 7:14*, the Lord demanded that His people "*...turn from their wicked ways.*"

Repentance is a turning from sin and self-reliance to the realization that God is the only hope for one's sinful condition. Jerald Daffe made the following observation in his book, *Revival: God's Plan For His People*:

> *Any claim of revival without confession of sin and a repentant heart is heresy. Also, there can be no claim of revival without a change in lifestyle. Lifestyle includes our beliefs, attitudes, appearances and actions. There can never be a revival of worship without a revival of confession and repentance.*

The desperate need of the hour in regard to revival is that of *genuine repentance.* A little boy in Sunday School was asked by his teacher if he could define the word *repentance.* His reply was, "*It means you are sorry for your sin.*" After he had finished his definition, a little girl spoke up and said, "*No sir, it means you are sorry enough to quit your sin.*" This is truly the Scriptural meaning of the word. It means that man will not continue in his rebellion towards God. *Repentance will not suffer people to make excuses for their sinfulness. Nor will it allow them to shift the blame to someone else.* Any movement that does not emphasize the doctrine of *true repentance* is not a movement that is sanctioned by God.

From *Genesis 1:1* to *Revelation 22:21*, there is a basic message of turning from sin. We need to experience personal, collective and national repentance. If we are not willing to turn from our sin, there is no hope whatsoever that God will give us the showers from Heaven that we so desperately need. If in fact revival does come, there must also remain within its participants an intense spirit of repentance, in order to perpetuate and sustain the revival blessings. J Wilbur Chapman, in his book, *Revival Sermons,* said:

> *I have been turning over the pages of the New Testament. I find that repentance is essential to forgiveness, that repentance is essential to possession of peace, and that repentance is essential to a final entrance into the city of God. I find over and over again the word repentance emphasized. The quickest way to have God remove His presence is to remain stubborn to His convicting power. Be zealous therefore and repent.*

Jesus is Lord

A third unmistakable theme of real revival is the great emphasis upon the *Lordship of Christ.* The Greek word *Kurios*, which means *lord* or *master*, is used over five hundred and fifty times in the New Testament in reference to Christ. No matter how hard one may try, they can't divorce the Lordship of Jesus Christ from the Bible. In real revival, the believer will be overwhelmed with a sense of belonging to God. They will ultimately realize that "*ye are not your own.*" (1 Corinthians 6:20)

There are two extremes in dealing with this crucial doctrine. One group says that man will know everything that there is to know about the Lordship of Christ at the point of salvation. Some even go as far to say that if one did not use the actual word *Lord* then they were not really saved.

The other view says that the believer can live his or her life any way they wish after they're converted. *Both of these views are wrong*. Man will not understand everything there is to know about the claims of Christ at the point of salvation. However, God requires that Christians, "*grow in grace and in the knowledge of our Lord and Saviour Jesus Christ" (*2 Peter 3:18).

The view that states man may live as he pleases is most certainly un-Scriptural. It only took the Apostle Paul a few moments on the Damascus Road to declare, "*Lord, what wilt thou have me to do?"* A simple study of the Word of God will quickly reveal that Christ is always the master, and the believer is always the servant.

The Lordship of Christ will be preached about and lived under during times of genuine refreshing from God, "*Every knee shall bow, and every tongue shall confess that Jesus Christ is Lord." (*Philippians 2:10) This will be the great understanding and burden of the hour.

Man has a very simple choice. He can give God everything he has, including his life, right now because he wants to, or he can yield it all in the day of judgment because he has to. Much more could be said on this subject; however, one thing is certain: Christ will be exalted as Lord, or man will be lost in spiritual darkness and depravity with no hope of the fire of God consuming the dross of his heart.

Hunger and Thirst for Righteousness
A fourth theme that is prevalent during seasons of revival is that of *hungering and thirsting after righteousness.* When God begins to move upon the hearts of His people, He brings them to a new level of spirituality. Christians begin returning to their first love. Hearts that have been cold and indifferent to the things of God are once again ignited with passion and zeal. The Word of God will suddenly become, "*the joy and rejoicing of the heart.*" (Jeremiah 15:16)

Prayer becomes a season of heavenly conversation, rather than a dull and much interrupted ritual. The recipients of revival will want to grow in grace to a greater degree. David said, "*I will be satisfied, when I awake, with thy likeness.*" (Psalm 17:15) He was not merely satisfied with knowing about his God, he wanted to get all of God that he could possibly handle.

Jesus reminds us, "*Blessed are they which do hunger and thirst after righteousness, for they shall be filled.*" (Matthew 5:6) The reason the churches, families and nations of the world are not overflowing with righteousness is simply because they are not interested in seeking after the things of God. Instead, they are full of the things of this world. The Lord promised His people through the mouth of Isaiah that He would, *pour water upon him that is thirsty.* (Isaiah 44:3) The simple prerequisite to receiving the blessing is being thirsty.

A historical study of the 1904-1906 Welsh Revival will reveal that the sale of Bibles and New Testaments increased at such an alarming rate that the publishing companies could not keep up with the great demand for the word of God. People were hungry to read, study, memorize and obey the truths of God's law. As revival continues to do its gracious work in the hearts and lives of those involved, time and daily schedules are forgotten, *Clock watchers* will never experience a genuine moving of the Holy Spirit.

God does not work on the level or the limits of man. "*His ways are not our ways, and His thoughts are not our thoughts.*" (Isaiah 55:8-9) It is true that organization and discipline are important factors in church schedules however, when the presence of God comes down among His people, the order of service will be done away with as believers seek more of the presence and power of God.

TIMEOUT: A Great Desire for the Things of God

Before proceeding with the six themes, it's important to further explain the crucial role of *hungering and thirsting* for the things of God. For that purpose, let's take a timeout to identify eight ways of identifying whether you or your church lack this sincere desire, and thereby are in desperate need of revival.

1. When there is no desire for the Word of God, revival is needed.

The Bible is a living book for living people. It is not designed to be black words on white paper. The Bible has the answer to all of life's questions and the solution to all of life's problems. In *2 Timothy 3:16-17* we read, "*All scripture is given by inspiration of God, and is profitable for doctrine, for reproof, for correction, for instruction in righteousness: That the man of God may be perfect, thoroughly furnished unto all good works.*" Without a doubt, this is one of the most cardinal passages of Scripture on the inspiration of the Bible.

The Apostle Paul states that ALL, not some, but the entire Bible is the God breathed pages of holy writ. He then goes on to say that the Word of God is *profitable.* Many people have the idea that the Bible is an outdated and antiquated book with absolutely no relevance to today's society. There could be nothing further from the truth. The

Bible is just as up to date today as it was when the ink-pen of inspiration ceased to write in *Revelation 22:21*. When a spirit of dullness and duty attend one's reading of such a sacred book, a quickening of the heart is definitely in order. As one writer of yesteryear has put it:

> *The Bible contains the mind of God, the state of man, the way of salvation, the doom of sinners, and the happiness of believers. Its doctrines are holy, its precepts are binding, its histories are true, and its decisions are immutable. Read it to be wise, believe it to be safe, and practice it to be holy. It contains light to direct you, food to support you, and comfort to cheer you. It is the traveler's map, the pilgrim's staff, the pilot's compass, the soldier's sword, and the Christian's character. Within its pages' paradise is restored, heaven is opened, and hell is disclosed. The LORD Jesus Christ is its grand object, our good is its design, and the glory of God is its end. Read it slowly, frequently, and prayerfully. Let it fill your memory, rule the heart, and guide the feet. It is a mine of wealth, a paradise of glory, and a river of pleasure. It is given you in life, will be opened in the judgment, and remembered forever. It involves the highest responsibility, will reward the highest labor,* ***and will condemn all who trifle with its sacred contents****.*

2. When there is a neglect of the House of God, there is a great need for renewal in the heart.

The place of worship is not for social status or personal gratification, it is for the corporate worship of God. R.A. Torrey had this to say:

> *Then, there is the increasing disregard for the Lord's Day. It is fast becoming a day of worldly*

pleasure, instead of a day of holy service. The Sunday newspaper with its mundane rambling and scandal has replaced the Bible. Visiting, golfing and bicycling have replaced Sunday School and the church service.

Our generation is in desperate need of believers that love and respect the House of God. In *Hebrews 10:25* we read, "*Not forsaking the assembling of ourselves together, as the manner of some is, but exhorting one another: and so much the more, as ye see the day approaching.*" This is obviously not a suggestion, rather a command.

Without a doubt, the New Testament Church would be absolutely ashamed at the way modern day Christians so tritely treat the fellowship of the local church. Revival must sweep through our churches and communities if we're ever going to restore the Church to the glory that it once had.

3. When a spirit of selfishness permeates your life, it reveals that a revival is needed.

We are commanded in Scripture to be givers and not takers. In times of real revival, the spirit of giving is greatly increased among Christians. The reason that so many people experience such a lack of financial substance is simply because God cannot trust them with what He gives them. A revival of sacrificial giving would meet needs that are right now going unmet. "*Give and it shall be given...*" (Luke 6:38)

4. When there is no desire or burden to see sinners converted, a revival is definitely in need.

We have been commanded and called by God to, "*Let the redeemed of the Lord say so*" (Psalm 107:2) It should not grieve a Christian to share his or her faith with an unbeliever. God has done too much for His children to have them discuss everything in society, yet never mention His saving grace.

5. When prayer is completely powerless, the need for revival is obvious.

The disciples asked of Christ that He would teach them to pray. One can be assured, He did not teach them to pray in a ritualistic fashion. Prayer is meant to have meaning and power for the child of God. When real revival begins to take place, believers have no greater joy than to fellowship with the great God of Heaven. In his book, *Fresh Power*, Jim Cymbala said this:

> *Revival comes when people get dissatisfied with what is and yearn for what could be. One of the distinguishing traits of the early church was their practice of serious prayer. The root problem is the need for the Holy Spirit to come in power and birth a true spirit of prayer. In other words, we must first secure the Spirit's presence and grace, then we can move out in powerful praying for all kinds of other needs. Prayer is the avenue God uses to come and bless His people; far more is accomplished by persevering in prayer than in taking charge of things myself.* Oh, how God's people need to pray. It has been well said, "*When we lay aside the power of prayer, we lay aside the power of God.*

6. When the desire for pleasure is predominant, a great revival is needed.

Most people, even in the Church, seem to be too busy for the things of God. Occasional enjoyments and amusements are by no means anti-Biblical, but to be dominated by fleshly appeals will choke the spiritual life out of any born again Christian. As the Lord begins to *rend the Heavens* believers will find themselves caught up in the whirlwind of God's glory instead of flocking to the next amusement to appease their ever-longing flesh.

7. When rebellion is regular, then an awakening is without a doubt the great need of the heart.
According to *1 Samuel 15:23*, "*Rebellion is as the sin of witchcraft.*" If in fact rebellion is continued and persisted in, the need of the heart is salvation and not revival. However, God's people can involve themselves in acts of disobedience and rebellion against their master. This rebellion must be repented of if one desires to draw closer to the Lord

8. When there is a lack of faith in God, there is a need for the Lord to manifest His presence.
Christians are to be people that live by faith and not merely by sight (2 Corinthians 5:7). *Hebrews 11:6* is a reminder that it is impossible to please God without faith. When the Church loses its confidence in a God that knows all and can do all, a revival of religion needs to be earnestly sought after. Much more could be said along these avenues of thought. However, it will suffice to say that an unavoidable hunger and thirst after the things of God will be greatly manifested in times of real refreshing.

Unity Among Believers
As we return to our review, the fifth theme of revival is *unity among believers.* On several occasions, the book of Acts records that the Church *had all things in common and* were *in one accord* (Acts 4:32). When true revival takes place, there will be a spirit of reconciliation and forgiveness among God's people. Longstanding accounts of bitterness will be removed as the heart is changed by the love and compassion of the Spirit.

Believers will enter into a loving and serving relationship with one another, placing value on the body and causing a fresh sense of unity and fellowship among its members. Malicious fighting, backbiting, gossiping and slanderous remarks will fade into the background, and gracious behavior will be the norm of the day. As we study historical awakenings and revival movements, we discover that even differing denominations were unified for the purpose of, and continuance of, revival. There are no denominational ties or super structures in the Bible.

They exist, however, because of the many personalities throughout Christendom. Let it be well stated; although revival can and has crossed over many a denominational boundary, a genuine working of God will never cross over a doctrinal boundary.

Years ago, all mainline denominations had a basic fundamental stand upon the Word of God. Through time, liberalism and modernism crept onto the religious scene and perverted the positions of these once sound Scriptural churches. The reason that revival is not sweeping across all the world's churches is simply because all the mainline denominations have gone completely apostate.

Malcolm McDow and Alvin L. Reid, in their Book *Firefall,* had the following to say in regard to doctrine during times of revival:

> *In times without revival the Church tends to move towards a humanistic philosophy, in revival the participants always make attempts to return to a simplified doctrine based on Biblical teachings. A strong emphasis upon the deity of Christ, His atoning death on the cross, His bodily resurrection, Biblical authority, the lostness of man, and the sufficiency of Christ to save sinners.*

If God ever sees fit to send a worldwide, or even a national revival, there will be a remnant of fundamentalists in all denominations that will band together for the common purpose of bringing glory to God. Regardless, if it deals with various churches in the same area, or if it is located within one church, revival will always bring about a forgiving and reconciling process. Hurts will be healed. Barriers will be removed. Prejudices will be overcome. When God comes down among His people in great power and glory, the many mountains of strained relationships will flow down at His presence.

Be Ye Separate

A sixth and final theme that all awakenings and revivals will emphasize is that of *separation.* Believers will come into a new level of holy and righteous living. Personal and ecclesiastical separation will be the normal atmosphere in any supernatural movement from Heaven. God told His people to, "*Come out from among them and be ye separate.*" (2 Corinthians 6:17) This statement is not a worthless suggestion; it is a straightforward command. God desires that His children live a different type of lifestyle than that of the world. *The blessing of God has always been upon separated Christianity,* God uses these seasons of refreshing called revival to bring His people into a more *peculiar* walk with Himself.

We are the l*ight of the world.* Lights are designed to shine bright throughout the darkness (Matthew 5:14-16). Believers should live a godly and separated life, so that their testimonies may shine to a lost and dying world. Dr. R.A. Torrey, in his work on *The Need Of General Revival*, said, "*In times of revival, Christians come out from the world and live separated lives, Christians who have been amused with the world and its pleasures give them up. These things are found to be incompatible with increasing life and light.*"

David R. Barmhart, in his book, *The Church's Desperate Need Of Revival*, said, "*There is no remedy under Heaven when people refuse to separate from evil.*

There will never be revival for an individual or a church where evil entanglements are willfully maintained."

He went on to give four ways in which God's people will be separated during times of revival. They are as follows:

1. *There will be a personal separation from all practices which are contrary to the Christian's new life in Christ, in order that the Holy Spirit may continue unhindered in the work of sanctification.*
2. *Christians will not only flee from evil, but also oppose it as a true soldier of the Cross.*
3. *Sanctification and holiness of life will be the standard for the fellowship of the Church.*
4. *False teachings and practices will not be tolerated in the Church.*

Any movement that does not major on a separated life, is most assuredly not a movement from God. "*God is light, and in Him is no darkness at all."* (1 John 1:5) As we press on, it's important to note that there are indeed other themes we could examine, but the six we explored in this chapter should suffice for this brief study. As we proceed to *Chapter Four,* we'll take a closer look at the actual markings of a legitimate revival among the people of God.

But ye are a chosen generation, a royal priesthood, an holy nation, a peculiar people; that ye should shew forth the praises of him who hath called you out of darkness into his marvellous light...

~ 1 Peter 2:9

4

Characteristics of Revival

There are many similar characteristics in a genuine moving of revival. Although locations and people may vary, God's workings among His people are very similar in nature. From the historical movements in the Old Testament, through the divine visitations of the New Testament Church, certain principles have been applied in all of God's dealings with man.

Spontaneous Nature

As we continue to study these various characteristics, we will find that, first and foremost, all revivals are of a *spontaneous nature***.** Webster's Dictionary defines the word *spontaneous* in the following ways:

1. *Occurring without apparent external use.*
2. *Impulsive: unpremeditated.*
3. *Unconstrained and unstudied in behavior.*
4. *Growing without cultivation or human labor.*

This is exactly what happens during revival! God comes down to the rescue of His people at unusual and unknown times. He begins to work at times and in places that we would never expect. We're reminded of Hezekiah's revival. The Bible says, "*...for the thing was done suddenly.*"

One may pray for revival over a period of twenty or thirty years; however, God can send revival in a matter of seconds. In regard to the Welsh Revival, Oswald J. Smith wrote the following: "*Suddenly, like an unexpected tornado, the Spirit of God swept over the land.*" When real revival breaks out it is with very little, if any, outside promotion or interference. Certainly, the Holy Spirit does not need radio announcements, handbills, newspaper ads or any other type of external promotional means. He is not confined to our church buildings, and most assuredly not to our well-organized services.

Genuine revival is usually not self-promoted. It is very noticeable in Scripture that Pentecost was promoted by the great works of God. It was not the campaigning skills of the apostles. The greatest advertisement for the Church is fire in the pulpit and fire in the pew. People will find themselves having irresistible urges to go to the House of God. The whole community will begin to speak of the supernatural work that God is accomplishing. It has often been said, "*Trying to dictate and control revival, is like trying to dictate and control the wind.*"

I.D.E. Thomas, in his book God's Harvest, *The Nature Of True Revival*, said:

> *It is impossible for anyone to plan a timetable or set a time-limit for a revival. No man can predict the day of its commencement, nor the hour of its termination. Just as the reaper remains in the field, far beyond the time of normal harvest, so a revival may continue unabated for many weeks or many months. With other programs, we normally*

announce the day on which they start, and the day in which they are to finish. Even our evangelistic campaigns have to conform to human timetables. But not so a revival; it refuses to comply with man-made schemes and remains immune to the dictates of committees.

The commencement and duration of revival is beyond human control. Everyone has seen brightly colored posters announcing Revival Meetings about to be held in a locality. We are told the exact date they are to start, and the exact date they are to finish. But this is presumption: sinners daring to claim the work of the Almighty! Only those profoundly ignorant of the working of the Holy Spirit speak of revival in this way. No one can tell, with any certainty, where revival will break out, it has often started in the most unexpected place, and amongst the most unlikely people.

A diligent study of how God has worked in the past will reveal that revivals have many times ceased almost as quickly as they started. The Lord uses these short and sometimes very long periods of renewal to prepare His soldiers for the future battles that they will face. Without a doubt, God cannot be placed in a box. In His sovereignty, He will work as He pleases. In an article entitled, *Thought Of The Revival Of 1858*, David N. Lord said, "*This advent was so sudden and heralded, that ministers were in many cases taken by surprise, and scarcely able to realize that an awakening was breathing on the hearts of their congregations.*"

When revival comes, it will not have to be manufactured or manipulated. The spontaneous outworking of the Holy Spirit will be all that is needed to sustain what God wills to accomplish. Jesus said, "*The wind bloweth where it listeth and thou hearest the sound thereof, but canst not tell whence it cometh and wither it goeth."* (John 3:8). This is a wonderful description of God's sudden great workings during revival.

Unbridled Emotions

A second characteristic of revival is that of the *displaying of emotions*. Different people will respond in different ways to God's convicting power. Emotional outbursts are common in all accounts of revival. J Edwin Orr put it well, when he said, "*During times of revival, the first person to wake up is the Devil."* The Devil is a master at counterfeiting and fabricating revival. When God begins to do something unusual in the hearts and lives of His People, the Devil will work with great mastery to thwart the moving of the Holy Spirit.

One of the most obvious ways in which he has done this is in the area of emotional manifestations. People will tremble, cry, remain on their faces and even shout for deliverance when God begins to reveal Himself and uncover their *secret sins.* (Psalm 19:12) However, the Devil tries to take this a step further, by having people bark like dogs, laugh uncontrollably, thrash around on the floor like a fish out of water and even claim to have been *slain in the spirit.*

There is absolutely nothing wrong with someone showing emotion during times of revival. Some people have an entirely different emotional make-up, and they tend to express it much more than others. When the outbursts of emotion become the center of attention, however, it can be rightly stated that it is of the spirit, but not God's Spirit. Jesus told His disciples that the Holy Spirit would not speak of Himself, rather, He would speak of things concerning Christ.

The ministry of the Spirit is not to promote Himself. It is to uplift and exalt Jesus. Any movement or organization that over-emphasizes the ministry and doctrine of the Holy Spirit has a very un-Biblical and unhealthy balance. *In real revival, Jesus Christ will be the center of attention.* He will be preached about from the pulpit and lived for in the pew. *All eyes on Jesus* will be the theological and practical mindset of the revival. Dr. A. W. Tozer, in his book, *The Pursuit Of God,* said the following in regard to Christ:

> *Wherever we turn in the church of God, there is Jesus. He is the beginning, middle, and end of everything to us. There is nothing good, nothing holy, nothing beautiful and nothing joyous, which He is not to His servants. No one needs to be poor, because if he chooses, he can have Jesus for his own property and possession. No one needs to be downcast, for Jesus is the joy of Heaven, and it is His joy to enter into sorrowful hearts.*
>
> *We can exaggerate about many things; but we can never exaggerate our obligation to Jesus or the compassionate abundance of the love of Jesus to all of us. All our lives long we might talk of Jesus, and yet we would never come to an end of the sweet things that might be said of Him. Eternity will not be long enough to learn all He is, or to praise Him for all He has done, but then, that matters not: for we shall be always with Him, and we desire nothing more.*

This is the true spirit of genuine revival. Brian H. Edwards, in his book, *Revival, A People Saturated With God,* had this to say, "*Though some should wish it the contrary, if we put all the recorded revivals together, we shall find that these 'phenomena' or unusual things, make up a very small part of the whole. Revival itself is unusual, and the great work of conviction, conversion and the creation of a holy life put all other things into the shade.*"

There has been much controversy through the years of church history over these emotional displays.

Jonathan Edwards and George Whitefield were not very sympathetic towards these outbursts of emotion in their services. John Wesley, Charles Finney and Evan Roberts, however, allowed the raw emotions of people to come out during all of their meetings.

When the theatrical displays of emotion became overemphasized, all of these men rebuked those who continued and persisted in exaggerated emotional upheavals. History records for us that during the world-famous sermon, *Sinners In The Hands Of An Angry God,* Mr. Edwards made attempts to quiet the emotions of the congregation in Enfield, Connecticut. It's worth repeating with emphasis: The conviction of the Spirit of God *will* bring about various reactions from differing people, but these outward showing of emotions *should not* be the central focus of the revival outpouring.

In an article entitled *The Necessary Ingredients Of A Biblical Revival,* Jan H. Murray wrote:

> *It is therefore a dangerous error to suppose that revivals have some unique ingredient by which their authenticity is to be judged. In times of alleged revival there may be extraordinary excitement: there may be many professions of faith: there may be striking physical phenomena and much emotion; strong men weep or fall to the ground like the jailer at Philippi, but not all these things together are, in themselves, proof that revival is genuine.*
>
> *Sometimes more is needed. The Biblical tests by which the normal work of the Spirit is recognized have to be applied and if that normal work is not found to be present, it is certain that, whatever men may claim, there is no Biblical revival.*

Heartfelt Singing of Praise
A third unmistakable mark of revival will be that of a *renewed and heartfelt devotion in singing.* Genuine revival turns a normal song service into a thriving and spirit-filled choir for the glory of God. People begin to sing with new fervor and zeal. No longer do they sing, *black words on white paper.* Accounts of the Welsh Revival of 1904-1906 shed much light on how singing is affected during a visitation from God. The Rev. R.B Jones, in his marvelous book, *Rent Heavens: The Welsh Revival Of 1904,* had this to say about our subject at hand:

> *The singing was truly magnificent and stirring. In the places of worship, the singing is not entrusted to a few who compose the choir. The whole congregation is the choir. No part in the harmony of a tune is missing, and most of the singers sing as ones trained. Imagine such an instrument with its very string swept by the breath of God in revival degree, unless heard it is unimaginable, and when heard, indescribable.*
>
> *There was no human leader, there was no hymn book; no one gave out a hymn. Anybody started singing. And very rarely did it happen that the hymn started, no one knew by whom, was it out of harmony with the mood of the meeting at the moment. No need for an organ. The assembly is its own organ, as a thousand sorrowing or rejoicing hearts found expression in the sacred psalmody of their native hills.*

If one were to attend many of the services of Gospel preaching churches throughout the land, it would be very evident that a spirit of revival is greatly needed based on the way the congregation is singing. Most of our Americanized church members flippantly and hypocritically sing to the Lord. When true revival begins to shine its rays of hope among God's people, the singing will be Spirit-led, Spirit-filled and Christ honoring. According to *Ephesians 5:18*, evidence that someone is *filled with the Spirit*, is the song that is in their heart. David said, "*He hath put a new song in my mouth, even praise unto our God..."* (Psalm 40:3) A real atmosphere of revival will be a real atmosphere of singing praises from the abundance of our hearts to our great and wonderful God.

Unusual Conviction

A fourth major characteristic of genuine revival is the *unusual way that people are brought under conviction.* Certainly, any man, woman, boy or girl that is brought to a saving knowledge of Jesus Christ must first experience Holy Spirit conviction. In times of revival, God uses even the smallest circumstances to bring sinners unto Himself and fan the flame of revival across the land.

Several historians of the 1904-1906 revival in Wales relate the following story: During a Sunday morning prayer service that was specifically designed for young people in the community, the pastor of the little church asked for testimonies regarding the spiritual lives of the teenagers that were present. Many began to speak on different themes. When one of them would speak too long, the pastor would kindly ask them to conclude for the sake of the others who perhaps wished to speak.

A young lady, who had been converted only a few days, rose to speak. With a trembling voice and shaking hands, she simply said, *"I love Jesus Christ with all of my heart."* The young ladies name was Florrie Evans, and God used this simple statement from her feeble lips to ignite the hearts of those that were present. Within a few short days, four neighboring towns and thousands of people were changed for the better because of the few simple words that were spoken from the mouth of this *babe in Christ* (Psalm

8:2). The Lord used these words as a sharp sword to slay the hearts of the indifferent. What a perfect illustration of God using, "*the weak things to confound the mighty.*" (1 Corinthians 1:27) In his book, *Accounts Of Religious Revivals in Many Parts Of The United States From 1815 To 1818, Joshua* Bradley recounts a remarkable conversion experience. The setting is Suffield, Connecticut in the spring of 1815, as he wrote:

> *The first instance of conversion was a young woman, who, like many others, had been very careless and vain. Retiring to rest one evening as she blew out her candle, the thought forcibly impressed her mind, that God could as instantly blow away her breath, and what then would become of her immortal soul. Her distress was great, and her conviction increased, until she enabled to resign her all into the hands of her blessed Saviour. She related her experience and obeyed her Lord.*

Revival history is full of these unusual and supernatural conversions. When God's Spirit begins to move with great convicting and convincing power, the subjects at hand are made to willfully bow themselves to His every dictate and commandment. It may be a particular phrase in a sermon. It may be the words of a familiar song. Perhaps it is through a conversation or in the pages of a book. No matter what He may see fit to use, know this: He will use whatever means necessary to break, tear, rend and mold hearts to accomplish His divine purpose.

The story is told of a man in Virginia Beach, Virginia. He had been convicted to go to church on many occasions but was reluctant and disobedient to do so. During a mighty sweep of God's hand in that area, his family was moving across town into another house, and were in the time-consuming process of rearranging their things. Each time he walked into the restroom; he would notice the manufacturer's name on the tank of the commode. The label simply read *Church.* The Lord used this simple word to send deep conviction to this man's heart. He was truly converted to Christ then and there and has now become an outstanding leader in his local church.

One further incident of historical significance will help to solidify our point. During the Hebrides Islands Revival of 1949-1953, God accomplished some remarkable things, and made trophies of grace out of many. The Rev. Duncan Campbell was God's revival instrument of choice. On the isle of Bernera, Mr. Campbell was assisting an assembly in a local church communion service. While he was preaching, there seemed to be a great heaviness and oppression over the congregation. The preaching seemed difficult. Realizing that Satan was desperately fighting to quench the fires of revival, Mr. Campbell stopped his message and called on a young man to lead in prayer. The young man's name was Donald Smith, and he was known for his simple, yet fervent prayers to God.

Donald rose to his feet and began his prayer. He alluded to the fourth chapter of the book of Revelation, which he had previously read that morning in his devotions he said, "*Oh God, I seem to be gazing through the open door. I see the Lamb in the midst of the throne, with the keys of death and Hell at His girdle."* At this point in his prayer, he began to weep very loudly. He then lifted his eyes toward the Heavens and cried, "*Oh God, there is power there, let it loose."*

With this simple act of bold faith, the Spirit of God swept through the congregation with tremendous force. One revival historian, David Smithers said, the church resembled a battlefield. The people began throwing their arms into the air and declaring over and over again, "*God has come, God has come."* Great conviction set in, and many people were brought to the grace of God.

Many others forsook sin, made restitution, and asked forgiveness for wrongs that had been done. When genuine revival comes, it doesn't take much for God to send an atmosphere of deep conviction to those who are involved. Unusual convictions and conversions are always a distinguishing mark of God's true work among His people.

A Changed Local Community

Within every revival that has ever taken place in the history of mankind, there is a fifth element by which one can judge the validity of the movement. *Has this revival changed the local community*? If the answer to the question is no, then it has obviously been worked up and fabricated by man. The study of revival will lead a person to empty saloons. It will take them to houses of prostitution that have been completely shut down. It will guide them through theaters that had to shut the doors because of a lack of patronage. When a genuine move of God makes its way into the hearts and lives of society, that society is changed.

The reason for this change in the land is simply because of the radical change in the heart. Revival brings with it a change in the Church as well. People begin to forget themselves, to forsake their sin, to be filled with the Spirit and to follow their Saviour. Marriages and homes are strengthened. In many cases, the Spirit of God sways entire nations.

In the seventeen hundreds, men like Jonathan Edwards and George Whitefield were very influential in steering America in the right direction. The Puritan influence helped in many ways, the moral climate of the nation. There are scores of historical awakenings that could be studied in great detail. Some of them are well known to all, and yet there are others that are known only to the small communities and towns that were privileged to experience such divine outpourings.

However, it will only take a brief study to reveal how God changes things when He begins to awaken His people. W.B. Riley said, "*sin is the tap-root of all social disorder. When the fire of revival begins to fall, sin will be dealt with properly. Therefore, social disorder will be greatly, if not completely, hindered.*"

The country of Wales mostly subsidized through the mining industry. During the two years of the Holy Spirits working there, many miners were converted to Christ. Almost every historian of the Welsh Revival cites the following incidents: The miners were worldly minded men. They didn't have much regard for others, and very little, if any, regard for God. During the days of revival, it is reported that these men were changed by the hundreds. Their faces would be streaked with white paths as the tears would run from their eyes and run a course down their cheeks.

As they would go back down into the mines, their lifestyle, language and mannerisms were different. On many occasions, the mining mules would not even respond to the commands of their master. The problem was not stubbornness, as some would think. It was simply because they could not understand the new vocabulary of the ones who had cursed them for so long. The swearing and filthy jokes were no longer a part of their daily routine. *God had come, and holiness had conquered.* In a message entitled, *The Nature Of A God-Sent Revival*, Duncan Campbell made the following observation:

> *In revival, when God and the Holy Ghost come, and the winds of Heaven blow, suddenly the community becomes God conscious! A God-realization takes hold of young, middle-aged and old. So that, as in the case of the Hebrides Revival, seventy-five percent of those saved one night were saved before they came near a meeting.*

Amazing as it may seem, revival does change entire cities. Evan Roberts had the unique privilege of seeing football teams disband because no one was going to the games. The people were saturated with God and had to go to the church house to meet with God. It was commonly reported that the jails were completely empty. In one town, there were no arrests or displays of public drunkenness for over a year. Several police officers put in for early retirement and formed *barber shop quartets* in order to sing at the various services in the many area churches.

In reference to God's great work in Wales, George T. B, Davis, in his book, *When The Fire Fell: How Prayer And Revival Can Save Our Country,* had this to say:

> *For the time being Wales had become the spiritual center of Christendom. Visitors from many lands flocked to Wales to witness the revival meetings, hoping, if possible, to carry back some revival fire to their own countries. Revival was the chief topic of conversation. The Welsh newspapers devoted columns to the movement each day; and occasionally special Revival Editions were issued*

What a miraculous difference God can make when He sends genuine revival! In 1835, Titus Coan was greatly used of God in a sweeping revival on the island of Hawaii. Little by little, the people came to hear him preach the Word of God. The people began to surround him so often that, as Oswald Chambers states it, "*Once he preached three times before he had a chance to take his breakfast.*" Revival had come, and the entire land was ablaze for God. The decision was made, and a two-year camp meeting was begun. Every day and night 2,000 to 6,000 people would gather to hear from Heaven. Weeping, shouting and loud continual sobbing was the norm of the day. When people would come to scoff at the meetings, God's Spirit would strike their hearts, and in almost every case they were converted.

The great Moravian Revival that began on August 13th, 1727 had lasting results for nearly one hundred years. John Wesley was mightily used of God in this revival. Society was changed for the better. Institutes for Biblical knowledge began springing up in many areas. There seemed to be a holy interest in every area of the society. Foreign missions were made a major priority, and thousands of dollars were raised for the missionary cause. Hundreds of hymns were written and composed during this time. Once again, God was shaping people, communities, and nations through the mighty power of revival. Eifion Evans, in his outstanding book, *Fire In The Thatch; The True Nature Of Religious Revival,* had the following to say in regard to the revivals of the eighteenth century:

> *In the experience of the Church, the eighteenth century was one continuous flow of revivals. The deadness and barrenness which had prevailed in the Church, and the indifference and immorality which had abounded in the world, could not withstand the surge of spiritual life which flowed through mere men, but issued from a divine source.*
>
> *Whole communities were affected and transformed, great churches were reformed, and invigorated, vast countries took on a new aspect. From this movement of God's Spirit, new missionary enterprises were born. The repercussions of the movement not only traversed continents, but also periods and ages, giving cause for generations to come to praise God, and securing for them a priceless heritage.*

Jonathan Edwards, in his work entitled, *A Faithful Narrative Of The Surprising Work of God in The Conversion Of Many Hundred Souls In Northampton, and The Neighboring Towns And Villages,* shed much light on this remarkable feature of revival. This is a rather lengthy quote, but it will greatly serve our purpose:

> *Presently upon this, a great and earnest concern about the great things of religion, and the eternal world, became universal in all parts of the town, and among persons of all degrees and all ages; the noise among the dry bones waxed louder and louder; all other talk but about spiritual and eternal things was soon thrown by. All the conversations in all companies and upon all occasions were upon these things only, unless so much as was necessary for people carrying on their ordinary secular business. Other discourse than on the things of religion would scarcely be tolerated in any company.*
>
> *Religion was with all sorts the great concern, and the world was only a thing by-the-by. The only thing in their view was to get into the Kingdom of Heaven, and everyone appeared to be pressing into it. There was scarcely a person in the town, either old or young, that was left unconcerned about the great things of the eternal world.*
>
> *Those that were want to be vainest and loosest, and those that had been most disposed to think and speak slightly of vital and experimental religion, were now subject to great awakenings. And the work of conversion was carried on in a most astonishing manner and increased more and more. Souls did, as it were, come by flocks to Jesus Christ.*
>
> *This work of God, as it was carried on and the number of true saints multiplied, soon made a*

> *glorious alteration in the town; so that in the spring and summer following 1745 the town seemed to be full in the presence of God: it never was so full of love, nor so full of joy; and yet so full of distress, as it was then. There were remarkable tokens of God's presence in almost every house. It was a time of joy and calmness on account of salvation's having been brought into them; parents rejoicing over their children as newborn, and husbands over their wives, and wives over their husbands.*
>
> *The goings of God were seen in the sanctuary; God's Day was a delight, and His tabernacles were amiable. Our public assemblies were then beautiful; the congregation was alive in God's service, everyone earnestly intent on the public worship. Every hearer was eager to drink in the words of the minister as they came from His mouth; the assembly in general was from time to time in tears as the Word was preached; some weeping with sorrow and distress, others with joy and love, others with pity and concern for the souls of their neighbors.*

Countless examples could be studied in regard to societal changes, but let's conclude with a statement by Owen Murphy in his book, *When God Stepped Down From Heaven*, "*Revival is an awareness of God that grips the whole community, the tavern and the roadside. The Church becomes a place where men find Christ.*"

Salvation of Souls

A sixth divine characteristic of Holy Ghost revival is the *salvation of souls.* People being saved is not revival, rather it is an *outflow* of real revival. Whenever there is a true spirit of revival, the evangelization of the lost will become a top priority. Revival is that which causes the believer to look inwardly at his own heart, whereas evangelism causes the believer to look outwardly at those who are perishing without Christ.

Drunkards, thieves, harlots, murderers, and adulterers will be brought under deep conviction of sin. People who have never heard the Gospel will willingly respond after the very first hearing. People who have rejected the Gospel for years will repent and be saved by the grace of God. As history records, revival has reached millions of souls for the Kingdom of God.

God's people have been told to, "*examine yourselves, to see whether ye be in the faith*" (2 Corinthians 13:5) This does not mean, however, that Christians should continually doubt their salvation. Once a person places their faith in Christ, they are eternally secure in Him. Even so, as the study of awakenings will reveal, scores of *professing* believers, church members, and religious people will be converted in the midst of a God-sent revival. Genuine revival has a way of making people lose their religious masks and get totally and brutally honest before God.

The hypocritical spirit of the Pharisees will be torn down. Sunday School teachers, church treasurers, bus drivers, laymen, deacons, and even preachers who have not genuinely been converted will fall beneath the pungent conviction of God's Spirit and be *born again.* It has often been stated, and rightly so, that probably fifty percent of today's professing church members have never really been saved.

George Whitefield was relentless and unsparing in his preaching on the necessity of ministers being converted. Such an issue would seem rather obvious, but these, "*Wolves in sheep's clothing"* (Matthew 7:15) were creeping into many of the churches in Whitefield's day, and he demanded that the ordaining committee perform a more thorough consultation of ministry candidates.

His personal journals record that countless numbers of ministers were saved during his revival efforts. Without a doubt, thousands of people being reconciled to God is an evident token that revival has and is taking place. *During the First Great Awakening, one out of every seven people in New England were converted to Christianity.* When God begins to move onto the scene and His divine presence is felt among the people, false conversions will most assuredly be brought out of the shadows and into light.

> *And that, knowing the time, that now it is high time to awake out of sleep: for now, is our salvation nearer than when we believed. The night is far spent, the day is at hand: let us therefore cast off the works of darkness and let us put on the armour of light.*
>
> ~ Romans 13:11-12

5

Revival: When Is "*Then*"?

In *1 Kings 18:38*, the Word of God says, "*Then the fire of the LORD fell...*" What was it that made God send His mighty fire down from Heaven? To answer that we would have to understand the spiritual backdrop for this portion of Scripture. Like all times that precede a great awakening, complete wickedness and apostasy were rampant. Ahab and Jezebel were the current leaders in control of the kingdom. They had absolutely no regard for Jehovah God whatsoever.

These were some of the most wicked leaders that Israel had ever known. Our great and majestic God is completely sovereign, and He does not need human instruments to fulfill His purposes. However, when He seeks to send revival, He always finds a man that He can entrust with such a divine moving. Many people will never experience revival for the simple reason that God cannot trust them with something so spiritual and holy, but in this epic time in the Biblical record, *God found just the man that He was looking for—the prophet Elijah.*

Principles Learned from Mount Carmel

There are five basic Biblical principles to revival that can be found through the study of the prophet Elijah that will help you understand what comes before the Lord will move in our midst. The first is needed now more than ever.

Calling Sin "Sin"

The *first principle* that allowed God to reveal Himself in great power at Mount Carmel was when Elijah *called sin by its proper name*. King Ahab had summoned for Elijah to stand in his presence. When Elijah refused to come, the king decided to go out and find him. When the confrontation began, the king blamed the man of God for the terrible drought that had been in the land for so long.

In *1 Kings 18:18*, Elijah said, "*...I have not troubled Israel; but thou, and thy father's house, in that ye have forsaken the commandments of the LORD, and thou hast followed Balaam.*" This mighty prophet did not soften his message. He preached hard on the fact that the king and the people had sinned in forsaking the commandments of God. Real revival will be saturated with the bold, unadulterated preaching of the Word of God. A wise preacher once said, "*The reason we have so many popsicles in the pew, is because we have so many polar bears in the pulpit.*" Red-hot preaching is what God has always blessed—and He always will.

Whatever happened to sin? What an appropriate question for this modern world in which we live. If we're going to have revival, sin must be denounced, and the holiness of God must be exalted. Today, preachers are fearful of preaching against specific sins. They're terribly afraid that they may lose their position, or worse yet, their salary. Years ago, preachers preached exactly what God had laid upon their hearts. They preached with a great burden and deep conviction. As a result, God began to move the hearts of the congregation. It's time we start getting this right.

The following four points outline how the Church in America has found itself as an integral part of a what Scripture calls a "*wicked and untoward generation.*" (Acts 2:40)

1. Sin has been relegated to nothing more than problems and habits.

People have actually begun to believe that their sin is only a mistake of character. Sin has now been renamed and certainly discolored. Drunkenness is now referred to as alcoholism. Sodomy is called an alternative lifestyle. Abortion is a woman's choice. And adultery is considered to be a simple extra-marital affair. Smoking, swearing, lying, and cheating are looked upon as ordinary habits. Dr. R.A Torrey said:

There is a lack of conviction of sin. Seldom are men overwhelmed with a sense of their own guilt in dishonoring the Son of God. Sin is regarded as a misfortune, infirmity, or even as good in the making. Seldom is it considered an enormous wrong against a Holy God.

Until people are willing to get honest before God about their sin, they will never experience genuine revival. David cried out, "*Against thee, and thee only have I sinned...*" (Psalm 51:4) Sin must be acknowledged, repented of, and forsaken. Making excuses for unrighteousness only pushes God's people farther from the work that He so wills to do. We must call it what it is; take no substitutes for it and have no mercy upon it.

2. Sin has been classified as "*big*" and "*little.*"
All sin is wicked and ungodly in the eyes of a thrice holy God. Although there are differing consequences of various sins, the Lord still condemns all unrighteousness. The Devil would have people believing in so-called *white lies* and black *lies.* The Bible truth is that man should not lie at all. There are no categories of sin with the Lord.

It is either right or wrong. Our ungodly flesh and the trickery of Satan keep us many times from seeing God really manifest Himself. Hundreds of people, and sad to say many believers, have the idea that because the times have changed, God has changed. Nothing could be further from the truth, *God never changes. If it was wrong one hundred years ago, then it is still wrong today.* Categorizing and classifying our sin will only broaden the gulf between man and revival. (Isaiah 59:2)

3. Sin has become something humorous and laughable.
Solomon reminds us in *Proverbs 14:9*, "*Fools make mock at sin.*" Our society is inundated with jokes, comics and comedians that jest over complete wickedness. Off color and shady jokes are a sure way to squelch God's Spirit during revival. *People in our day scoff at the God of Heaven and laugh with the demons of hell* when a true spirit of revival and conviction come among the children of God, they will be weeping over their sin, not laughing at their sin!

4. Sin has become commonplace in the Church of Jesus Christ.
It is no longer a great shock to the Church when we hear of someone *falling* into sin. It is nothing to see the Church acting in many ways like the world. The

> Spiritual decline of today's churches is lukewarm and indifferent. Apathy is on every hand, and around every corner. Sin used to shock us and keep us up at night. We used to fear God and hate evil but now, *the Church has seen, heard, and involved itself in so much sinfulness that it is an everyday occurrence, when it should be an everyday abhorrence.*

I remind you that the fire of God never fell upon the mountain until Elijah was first willing to call sin by its proper name, and it will not fall upon the Church until we do the same.

Standing Against the Forces of Hell

The *second principle* that made way for the fire of God to fall from Heaven was when the prophet of God *stood against the forces of hell.* A careful study of this portion of Scripture will reveal that Elijah was at the base of the mountain with eight hundred and fifty false prophets. All the people of Israel were there as well. These prophets of Baal were nothing more than Devil worshipers. The man of God was standing against all the powers of the wicked One. It must be remembered, when one stands against the forces of hell, all of Heaven stands with them.

In *1 John 4:4* we are told, "*greater is he that is within you, than he that is in the world.*" Again, the Lord Jesus states in *John 16:33*, "*In the world ye shall have tribulation, but be of good cheer, for I have overcome the world.*" The child of God does not need to fear their foes, nor their future (Romans 8:31). God has already promised His people the victory. We must be willing to take some ridicule for the cause of Christ, and for the sake of revival.

If a person is not willing to stand up against the Devil and his demons and allow God to use them as a channel of awakening, then that person, and perhaps many other people under their influence, will never experience revival. The Devil is always going to fight to stop real revival. If God's people desire revival, then we're going to have to fight the world, the flesh, and the Devil with unmerciful force.

Great Faith

The *third principle* that we see was Elijah having *exercised great faith.* After the prophets of Baal had prophesied and called upon the name of their god, it was Elijah's turn to prove the power of his God. The false prophets had been crying from early morning, until the time of the offering of the evening sacrifice. In *1 Kings 18:30*, we see that Elijah, "*...repaired the altar of the LORD that was broken down.*" He then asked the people to retrieve twelve barrels of water. The water was then poured all over the sacrifice, altar, and filled the trench round about.

To the people, it would seem that Elijah was making it much more difficult for his God to answer by fire. However, *Elijah realized that nothing was too difficult for his great God. The atmosphere for real revival is many times ruined by an unwillingness to put God to the test, Hebrews 11:6* attests to this by saying, "*Without faith it is impossible to please God.*" The world says that seeing is believing, but God's people realize that believing is seeing. Although genuine revival can't be manufactured or brought down from Heaven, one can be assured of the fact that it will never come unless we believe that God can send such a remarkable movement.

God commands that His people trust Him. If we don't have faith that God can send an old-fashioned revival, then we're disobedient to the clear commands of Scripture. An attitude of anticipation and expectation is essential in dealing with revival. We should not only have the faith that God *can* send revival but expect that He *will* send revival.

Hosea 10:12 says, "*Sow to yourselves in righteousness, reap in mercy, break up your fallow ground for it is time to seek the LORD, till He come and rain righteousness upon you."* This verse shows a very important element in regard to faith, expectation and revival. Hosea said that we are to seek the LORD for revival *until* He sends it. *The verse does not conclude that He will send revival. It does tell us, however, that we have a responsibility to seek it and desire it until it comes.*

In Edward E. Hindson's book, *Glory In The Church The Coming Revival*, he makes a simple yet profound statement along this line of thought, "*God will work in His sovereign time, but He will work! Do not be afraid of a lack of faith. Rather, be bold and expect great things...real faith believes and receives."* Elijah was a man that expected great and miraculous things from the hand of God, and consequently got what he was looking for.

Charles G. Finney had the belief that revival was basically nothing more than the proper use of the proper means. If in fact this is true, then revival could be promoted anytime and anywhere. A simple study of God's Word concerning revival would reveal the faulty logic of this interpretation. Man must have faith in God, and *expect* God to move, and this is expressed only by praying and seeking God's face.

Man must desire for God to move in unusual ways. However, none of this says that God is *required* to send revival. God is not so small that He can be put in a box of our making. The words of William Carey, the great missionary, can best illustrate our point. During an address to many prospective and veteran missionaries, he said the following: "*Attempt great things for God, expect great things from God."*

The Virtue and Necessity of Fervent Prayer

The *fourth principle* that preceded the fire of God falling was when *Elijah fervently prayed for God to move.* The prophets of Baal prayed for about twelve hours. A long day of prayer without one single answer. When Elijah began to call on the name of the LORD, he simply uttered sixty-three words of fervent prayer. His prayer was nothing of entertaining value. His words were not the least bit flamboyant or impressive to the ear.

Elijah realized the desperate situation he was facing. He also realized that God was going to have to move, and he prayed to that end. Prayer has always been a vital part of revival. The great commentator, Matthew Henry said, "*Whenever God intends great blessings for His people, He first sets them to praying.*" Revivals, awakenings, renewals, and prayer all go hand-in-hand. We know that God can do anything He pleases, yet—even so—God has bound Himself to perform certain events of supernatural proportion. This *covenant* or *binding* is not to everyone, but it is to those who pray.

2 Chronicles 7:14 says, "*If my people which are called by my name, shall humble themselves, and **PRAY**, and seek my face, and turn from their wicked ways: then will I hear from heaven, and will forgive their sin, and will heal their land.*" The conditions for the blessing were humility, prayer, seeking the face of God and repentance. God requires that His people get a burden for revival, and then act on that burden by beseeching the throne room of Heaven with earnest prayer.

Dr. Vance Havner once said, "*The situation is desperate, and the saints are not.*" There has never been a revival in all the history of revivals that did not start with prayer. On the day of Pentecost, the people were gathered in the Upper Room. In *Acts 1:14*, the Bible says, "*These all continued in one accord with prayer and supplication….*" They were unified for the common purpose of asking God to send His blessed, promised Spirit among them. Jesus had already told them that the Spirit was coming, but they insisted upon fervently praying until they received it.

Jonathan Edwards said, "*We must plead for explicit agreement and visible union of the people of God in extraordinary prayer for the revival of religion and the advancement of Christ's Kingdom."* In *James 5:16*, we have an example of the prophet Elijah, "*The effectual, fervent prayer of a righteous man availeth much."* If God says that effectual (energized) and fervent (boiling) prayers avail (accomplish) much, does it not stand to reason that if we effectively and fervently pray for God to send a mighty revival, that those prayers will accomplish much as well?

Christians must not take for granted the miraculous power of prayer. Prayer in the Word of God is always accompanied by the power of God. "*Little prayer equals little power. Much prayer equals much power. No prayer equals no power."* Dr. R.A Torrey, in his work on, *Prayer Before And During Revivals,* had this to say:

> *One of the great secrets of the superficiality and unreality of many of our modern, so-called revivals is that more dependence is put upon man's machinery than on God's power. His power must be sought and obtained by earnest, persistent and believing prayer. We live in a day characterized by the multiplication of man's machinery and the decrease of God's power. The great cry of our day is work, new organizations, new methods, and new machinery. The great need of our day is prayer.*

Dr. John H Rice, in a sermon entitled, *The High Cost Of Revival,* said:

> *God gives revivals. God gives them on exactly the same terms He ever gave them. God answers prayer. He is just as glad to answer prayer as He ever was. I say, God is the God of revivals. God has the same old-fashioned requirements for revivals*

> *that He ever had. If you want to find God, you can find Him, provided you search for Him with all your heart.*

An elderly saint in Texas, whose name has never been recorded, made the following statement: "*The only place you will ever find power coming before prayer, is in the dictionary.*" Let's look at an amazing example of how God has shaped revival and consequently history through prayer.

Jeremiah Calvin Lanphier was born in 1809. He lived in New York City and was a faithful member of the Old North Dutch Reformed Church on Fulton Street. As a single lay missionary, he was constantly on personal visitation, conducting street meetings and praying for others. Lanphier's heart was greatly burdened about intercessory prayer, especially for revival. Samuel Prime, in his book, *The Power Of Prayer: The Revival Of 1858,* tells of how the great burden for prayer was originated in his heart. The following quote is from Prime's book, but in the words of Lanphier himself:

> *Going my rounds in the performance of my duty one day, as I was walking along the streets, the idea was suggested to my mind that an hour of prayer, from twelve o'clock to one o'clock. would be beneficial to businessmen, who usually in great numbers take that hour for rest and refreshment. The idea was to have singing, prayer, exhortation, relation of religious experience, as the case might be that none should allow or require, or their inclinations dictate. Arrangements were made, and at twelve o'clock noon, on the twenty-third day of September 1857, the door of the story lecture-room was thrown open.*

His heart was overflowing to see God move amongst the men of the city. In many other records, we find that he made two observations that drove him to prayer. First, he noticed the great throngs of businessmen on the streets between twelve o'clock and one o'clock in the afternoon.

Second, he realized that if God would give him a thousand lifetimes, he would never have the ability to reach them all with the Gospel. Upon receiving this great burden from the Lord, he spoke with the church board about his idea. The members were not very excited about the idea but decided to allow Lanphier to proceed with his burden.

He began to aggressively promote the upcoming prayer meeting. He printed and distributed a handbill that announced the meeting. On the front of the handbill was the heading: "*How often shall I pray?*" Beneath the heading was the simple answer to this thought-provoking question, *"As often as the language of prayer is on my heart: as often as I see my need of help as often as I feel the aggression of a worldly spirit. In prayer, we leave the business of time for that of eternity and intercourse with men for intercourse with God."* On the backside of the handbill, he wrote:

> *A day prayer meeting is held every Wednesday from twelve o'clock to one o'clock in the Consistory building in the rear of the Old North Dutch Church, corner of Fulton and Williams streets. This meeting is intended to give merchants, mechanics, clerks, strangers, and businessmen generally an opportunity to stop and call on God amid the perplexity's incident to their respective vocations. It will continue for one hour, but it is designed for those who find it inconvenient to remain more than five or ten minutes, as well as for those who can spare a whole hour. Necessary interruption will be slight because it was anticipated. Those in haste*

often expedite their business engagements by halting to lift their voices to the throne of grace in humble, grateful prayer.

On the first day, Lanphier prayed alone for thirty minutes. Another man came to join him, and by the end of the hour there were six men in attendance at the meeting. The following Wednesday, there were twenty men. The third Wednesday, there were between thirty and forty men in attendance. After the third meeting, the men decided to begin to meet daily instead of weekly. The Lord began to graciously work in their midst. *The people began to yield themselves and God began to reveal Himself.*

Simultaneously, prayer meetings were started all across the city. Many of these meetings were started with no idea that Lanphier had begun a prayer gathering. The Lord was burdening His people to pray and pray they did. They desired that God would, "*pour them out a blessing which they could not contain.*" (Malachi 3:10) Within the first six months, it is recorded that fifty thousand people were meeting together for prayer in New York City every day of the week.

This great number of people does not include the hundreds of men and women who had begun to pray in other cities. As a young preacher, the great American Evangelist, D.L. Moody was greatly influenced by one of these prayer meetings. This great emphasis on prayer spilled over into other states and spread rapidly across the major cities in America.

There is some debate whether the Southern states experienced much of these revival blessings. If they did, it is certainly not documented. This lack of revival blessing from the hand of God was probably due to the wickedness of slavery, that was still very much alive in the South at that time. One miraculous thing about this revival was the fact that it was not confined to the United States. It shook people throughout Africa, England, France, Ireland, the British Isles, Scotland, New Guinea, and many other parts of the world.

What started as a city-wide prayer meeting, turned out to be a worldwide awakening. Although God burdened the heart of Lanphier to begin these meetings of prayer, this is the only recorded major revival movement that did not have one particular spiritual leader. *This movement was completely organized and energized by the Spirit of God.* It was then carried around the world by regular church laymen. That is why this revival has also been called The Layman's Prayer Revival. For an in-depth study on this wonderful moving of God, read in full J. Edwin Orr's book, *The Event Of The Century.* It is without a doubt the greatest treatment of this mighty move of God.

Prayer and revival cannot and must not be separated. W.B. Riley wrote a book entitled, *The Perennial Revival*. In it, he said, "*If the churches desire the return of revival as was on the day of Pentecost, then, as the people thereof, we must pray.*"

The conditions of an open Heaven have not changed much in many centuries. Evan Roberts had prayed for thirteen years before revival broke out upon the land of Wales. Pastor William McColloch prayed fervently for over a year before God met with his congregation in Cambuslang, Scotland in February of 1742.

Jonathan Edwards prayed with great intensity for three solid days and nights before he attempted to preach his sermon, *Sinners In The Hands Of An Angry God.* George Whitefield, John and Charles Wesley, Richard Baxter, Ashael Nettleton, the Tennets, Duncan Campbell, John Hyde, Charles Finney, David Brainerd, and a host of others were great men of revival, *but before they were great men of revival, they were first great men of prayer.*

Prayer is the spiritual engine that drives the magnificent vehicle of revival across the land. We have spent a great deal of time on the matter of prayer in regard to revival. Let's summarize by using a quote from Dr. Martin-Lloyd Jones, in a sermon entitled, *Revival: An Historical And Theological Survey.* With reference to those who participated in past revivals, he says:

> *They waited upon God and cried and cried until He did rend the Heavens and come down. Let us lay hold upon Him and plead with Him to vindicate His own truth and the doctrines which are so dear to our hearts, that the Church may be revived, and masses of people may be saved.*

Now, we come to the fifth and final principle that Elijah followed to incur the blessings of God.

Absolute Obedience

When Elijah stood in *absolute obedience* to God, it was then that the fire fell. In *1 Kings 18:36*, Elijah said, "*... I have done all these things at thy word."* This little statement at the end of the prophet's prayer implies that he had simply, yet willingly, obeyed the direct commands of God. He did not argue. He was not worried about his reputation with the crowd. He was more than willing to suffer ridicule for the cause of his God. Jesus said to His disciples, "*If ye love me, keep my commandments."* (John 14:15)

A true test that must be taken if we want the blessings of revival is simply: Do we obey God? A person who enjoys doing everything his or her own way is a person who will never experience revival. Obedience is the litmus test for love and desire. Obedience has always been a prerequisite to God's blessings. The Lord told the Israelites that He would *bless them* if they obeyed, but He would *curse them* if they disobeyed.

Evan Roberts, the human leader of the Welsh Revival, preached on what became commonly known as the Four Points. These points were as follows:

1. Is there any sin in your past that you have not confessed to God?
2. Is there anything in your life that is doubtful?
3. Do what the Spirit prompts you to do.
4. A public confession of Christ as your Saviour.

These are definitely points to be pondered. God used these simple questions, and statements to convict the hearts and lives of thousands. However, let's look in detail at point number three. In a message concerning the obedience of Abraham, Roberts intertwined the following:

> *Obedience: prompt, implicit, unquestioning obedience to the Spirit....We all ought to obey God as Abraham obeyed Him...We should give obedience instantly. Everyone must obey and go where God directs him. If we are the children of God, let us obey...Obey Him! Rest upon Him. The great lesson is obedience, obedience, obedience.... If we speak of the Spirit, we must obey the Spirit, and from doing that, great results are to occur. Though the whole world sneer at me, I know that I must obey the Spirit. When Abraham obeyed God, he was blessed.*

It is very obvious that Mr. Roberts believed in complete obedience to God. If we desire to see the great and mighty hand of God moving in our midst, we must be willing to obey, no matter what the cost. When Elijah did all of these fundamental things that we have discussed: *called sin by its proper name, stood against the forces of hell, exercised great faith in God, fervently prayed for God to move and completely obeyed God,* the fire fell out of Heaven and God was glorified. THEN, THEN, THEN.... When? Not until these other things were done did God send revival. If we really want revival, we must meet God on His terms.

The Lord, He is God

In 1 *Kings 18:39*, we see the response of all the people. The Bible says, "*And when all the people saw it, they fell on their faces: and they said, the LORD, he is the God; the LORD he is the God.*" The people put God in His proper place when the revival fires came. In all true revivals, God will be uplifted, exalted, and glorified. The major Bible text for real revival is *John 3:30*, *"He must increase, but I must decrease."*

In *1 Kings 18:40*, the Bible declares that Elijah had all the prophets of Baal taken down to the brook Kishon, and he "*slew them there.*" These idol worshipers were done away with after God moved amongst the people. They simply could not, and would not, tolerate false gods and wicked idols after the revival came. In the midst of genuine revival, idols will be torn down, and God's people will have to take a little trip to the river and slay some false prophets that have taken up residence in their lives.

> *But there were false prophets also among the people, even as there shall be false teachers among you, who privily shall bring in damnable heresies, even denying the Lord that bought them, and bring upon themselves swift destruction.*
>
> ~ 2 Peter 2:1

CONCLUSION

As we bring our simple study of revival to a close, we will conclude with an excerpt from a sermon by Dr. Vance Havner. As he neared the end of his very fruitful ministry, he preached a stirring sermon from Revelation Chapter two entitled, *Christ's Call to Revival.* This brief quote will best serve our purpose as we conclude our study of this most sacred subject:

> *Perhaps nothing is more cluttered with false notions and contradictory ideas than the matter of revival. More energy has been misdirected, more carts put before the horse on this theme, than almost any other that engages our attention. A revival is not an evangelistic campaign, it is not a church paying out of debt or erecting a new building or putting on a stewardship campaign. These things may flow from revival, but they do not constitute one. A revival is not a drive for church members. A revival is a work of God's Spirit amongst His own people...*
>
> *A lot of so-called joy of the Lord is merely whipped emotion, which leaves a lot of unconfessed sin and hidden iniquity. We have made convalescents of church members who need operations. We have tried to cure them with sunshine, leaving the focal infection untouched....*
>
> *Men will not desire a physician until they know they are sick, and they will not seek a closer walk with God so long as they are content to get along without it. There is, however, a wrong emphasis in preaching on revival. Sometimes it has created the*

impression that revival is a spurt of religious enthusiasm which is not possible to live up to year-round. As a matter of fact, what we call revival is simply New Testament Christianity, ***the saints getting back to normal.***

But seek first the kingdom of God and his righteousness, and all these things will be added to you.

~ Jesus (Matthew 6:33)

A REVIVAL POEM

I now have ashes
Where I once had fire
The soul in my body seems dead
The things I once loved
I now merely admire
My heart is as gray as my head
Our service for God has been barren and dry
And barren it shall remain
Until we are blessed with fire from on high
And the sound of abundance of rain

Wilt Thou not revive us again, that Thy people may re-joice in Thee?

~ Psalm 85:6

Made in the USA
Monee, IL
22 May 2022

57f9e234-9492-4901-b1b7-09f7b6c22735R01